A HYPNOTIST'S JOURNEY FROM THE TRAIL TO THE STAR PEOPLE

By Sarah Breskman Cosme

Other books by the author:
- A Hypnotist Journey to Atlantis; available in Spanish and Latvian.
- A Hypnotist Journey to the Secrets of the Sphinx.

A Hypnotist Journey to Atlantis and A Hypnotist Journey to the Secrets of the Sphinx provide information obtained through various subjects by hypnotic past-life regression.

1. Hypnosis   2. Reincarnation   3. Past-life regression

4. Metaphysics   5. Hidden Secrets   6. Ancient History

I. Sarah Breskman Cosme

Cover Design: Amy Tripp

Book set in: Times New Roman

ISBN: 9798366851459

You've all forgotten that you incarnated to fulfill a long ago promise made to yourself, the promise of liberation. Liberation can only come when you abandon yourself to the complete dictation of the compassionate heart. When you allow the surrender, you will see the truth, the depths, and the expressions of this magical experience. Both are majestic and mundane, shallow, and deep. In this way you will finally liberate yourself and become a true steward of the world. Every life has a purpose, a plan, but realize that the only reality, the only real purpose, and the only thing that matters in the long run is the sincere cultivation of divine love.

–The Higher Self

A BRIEF OVERVIEW OF THE TERM
(THE TRAIL OF TEARS)

Trail of Tears, in U.S. history, the forced relocation during the 1830s of Eastern Woodlands Indians of the Southeast region of the United States (including Cherokee, Creek, Chickasaw, Choctaw, and Seminole, among other nations) to Indian Territory west of the Mississippi River. Estimates based on tribal and military records suggest that approximately 100,000 indigenous people were forced from their homes during that period, which is sometimes known as the removal era, and that some 15,000 died during the journey west. The term Trail of Tears invokes the collective suffering those people experienced, although it is most commonly used in reference to the removal experiences of the Southeast Indians generally and the Cherokee nation specifically. The physical trail consisted of several overland routes and one main water route and, by passage of the Omnibus Public Lands Management Act in 2009, stretched some 5,045 miles (about 8,120 km) across portions of nine states (Alabama, Arkansas, Georgia, Illinois, Kentucky, Missouri, North Carolina, Oklahoma, and Tennessee).

The roots of forced relocation lay in greed. The British Proclamation of 1763 designated the region between the Appalachian Mountains and the Mississippi River as Indian Territory. Although that region was to be protected for the exclusive use of indigenous peoples, large numbers of Euro-American land speculators and settlers soon entered. For the most part, the British and, later, U.S. governments ignored these acts of trespass.

Note to the reader: The information within this book may be triggering, sensitive and controversial. It is my great hope that this book acts as a catalyst for your own healing. The information is gathered from Quantum Healing Hypnosis sessions and thus I do not censor this information. In order to increase the validity of this information, I use multiple hypnosis subjects and clients who have no previous conscious knowledge of this information or of the other people. In this way, I try my best to present this information the way it has been presented to me. These books are truly written by the Higher Self of my subjects and clients while they are deeply under hypnosis. The Higher self of these clients has claimed that there is an agenda, and that is to get this information to those who need it. So, if you have found this book, or most likely this book has found you, strap on your seatbelts, and get ready for a wild ride.

INTRODUCTION

I don't know how I manage to stay skeptical after all the journeys I have taken, from the lessons I have learned from the secrets of the Sphinx to the forgotten histories of Lemuria and Atlantis; but still, after all of this, I yearn for that same momentum, that odyssey of a new story that, as with my past two books on these subjects, has taken me on such a wild ride that I have no choice but to let go and see where it leads. While I am truly grateful for what I have discovered, I am still hungry for more, more truths, more forgotten histories, more inspiring experiences that show the power of our souls, even at their breaking point.

A few weeks before this book officially started, a client's higher self, while under hypnosis, started talking about a new manifestation practice that I knew I needed to try. In this practice, the higher self said that you can manifest anything through emotions, because while a human experiences emotion, there are portal openings which contain countless possibilities. My client was told to feel a strong positive emotion, like happiness, and then to immerse himself in this emotion, visualize the portal opening, and then imagine pulling whatever it was he desired toward him from within this portal. I had just decided to give this a try; in fact, my eyes were still closed when my phone pinged. I don't know what surprised me more, the fact that my phone pinged while it was set to silent or the fact that it was from someone I had never met, named Les. Les claimed that for some strange reason she felt the urge to contact me, and even though that might sound crazy she said, she messaged me anyway and said she felt there was something she needed to tell me but wasn't sure what it was.

Some may call it a simple coincidence, but I recognize these small miracles as they happen, and quickly worked to get Les in for a session. As I put her under hypnosis for the first time, it became truly apparent that a new story had eagerly surfaced, needing to be told. Somehow, Les had found me. The universe had literally dropped my next subject into my lap.

TABLE OF CONTENTS

ACKNOWLEDGMENTS

Thank you to all my friends and family for your love and support.

Thank you, Dolores Cannon, and Julia Cannon, for your help throughout this book.

Thank you, to all my clients for letting me share your stories that made this book possible.

Thank you from the bottom of my heart to Les and Aniwaya, without whom this story would never have been shared.

Dear reader, this book is dedicated to you.

CHAPTER 1:
LES

Les, a young Caucasian woman in her late twenties nervously sat down for her first hypnosis session not knowing what to expect. As she easily drifted into deep hypnosis a surprising thing occurred. Les started talking in another voice that was more masculine and had a different tone to it.

L: They call me Aniwaya, this voice said through Les. I am the one who contacted you. I've been watching you because you needed to gain our trust first. You have proven yourself ready, and so, now I'm ready. I'm ready to tell our story.

I had goosebumps all over my body when this person named Aniwaya started talking through Les. I've had other voices come through clients before when they are deep under hypnosis, but this voice was different; it had what sounded to me like a Native American accent.

S: *Why did you contact me?*

L: I have been waiting for the right time to tell this story, to share this information. This information is key to helping humanity at this time and this isn't just our story, this is everyone's story. This is a special time for humanity, a time of uncovering; a time of embracing the shadow, of understanding your true history and of finally coming back together with this knowledge that we share.

S: *Who are you in relation to Les?*

L: I am what you would call a "past life" of hers, but understand that really this is a parallel life, as all time is not linear.

S: *What do you mean by that?*

L: Our soul doesn't go completely into one body. It is so large and so vast that in order for us to gain the most experience, our essence is divided. Everything that has ever happened in the past or ever will happen in the future is happening simultaneously right now. Time is just a social construct and doesn't work in a linear fashion the way your culture would think it does. Within this lifetime as Aniwaya that I speak to you from, I have chosen the job of communicator, and so I feel best suited for this task, to tell our story.

S: *How are you talking with me exactly?*

L: I'm currently in a focused meditation, a meditation that I have learned through many lifetimes.

S: *Could you explain how you put yourself into this meditation?*

L: By making my mind and my body very still I can focus deeply, and I can speak to you through Les. I have also raised my vibration, which makes this process easier, through harmonizing with nature and a lifelong practice of gratitude.

S: *Could you tell me more about how exactly you speak through her?*

L: This is almost like a phone call, but one where both of us have to concentrate and connect to get a clear connection.

S: *Tell me more about yourself.*

L: I was born into a tribe we called the "Wolf Tribe." I was not only raised with wolves, but I lived amongst them. Our wolf friends were beautiful teachers that reminded us that we are all part of the same consciousness that every living thing on the Earth shares. In my tribe we had a very deep understanding of the Earth and the universe, and we understood that every living being made a difference. Every being has a role in the intricate web of the universe.

S: *Did you have a role within your tribe?*

L: I have become a mediator, a communicator for my people.

S: *Why is now the time to tell your story?*

L: This is the time that has been foretold by the ages, a time of coming back together from separation. Although this time is chaotic, it is also a time of justice, a time when the collective shadow comes to light, and through this information, the world can remember who they really are. Throughout our story, we suffered great sadness, but it was the oneness of our tribe that allowed us to keep going, even through the worst of times.

S: *Can you start from the very beginning of your story, the story you wish to tell?*

L: I love to remember the beginning. The earliest parts of my life were the most fun because it was before it all happened.

S: *Tell me about it.*

L: Well in the beginning my village was beautiful. There was always a comfortable feeling of home in my village with a sweet smell of ash and burnt wood in the air from the fire that always brought happiness to me as a child. The fire is where we got together to share, dance, and play. Everything about my childhood was beautiful. We would dance under the stars, we would pray, and we were very much connected and supported by our natural environment and the People from the Stars who helped us always.

S: *Who are the People from the Stars?*

L: The beings from which we have descended. The Star People are the ones that guide us, that give us knowledge, that assist us. They are the ones who were responsible for giving us corn so that we could survive our winters. Corn has so much fat in it that when the winters come, we have enough fat on our bodies to be able to withstand it, along with our clothes and our other gear.

S: *Tell me more about your childhood there.*

L: When I think about my childhood, I think about the moccasins that my mother made for me. They were made with a very soft deer skin, and she always said that she sewed love into them, and I could feel the love in them because they always kept my feet warm. Even in the coldest deepest snow my feet were always warm.

S: *What did you wear on your body?*

L: I wore clothes that were also made of soft deerskin, and I wore many beads that decorated my clothes and fox fur on my wrists to keep my hands warm. Even at a young age I kept dried herbs in a medicine pouch that I wore around my neck always.

S: *What did you carry in your medicine pouch?*

L: Dried herbs, berries, and tobacco. We understood that nature provided us with a cure for any ailment and so we dried and used herbs for healing, pain, sleeplessness, and immunity.

S: *Tell me more about what it was like as a child there?*

L: When I was a child and before it all happened, I remember how fun it was to be a child there and how carefree we all were. There were many other children to play with and we were all very close. (Les began to laugh loudly) I gave one of my friends the nickname of Black Fox and we all thought that it was so funny! It was a joke because we're from the wolf clan!

S: *Tell me about him.*

L: Black Fox was smaller than the rest of us, but he was very quick on his feet and a clean shot with his bow. He was also my best friend.

S: *What is your family like?*

L: Our families are different from yours because everyone in our tribe is considered our family. We are all very close, compassionate, and caring for one another, but we have a matriarchal society, and it would be correct to say that mothers in the tribe were celebrated and that is how I considered my mother. She was the most important person to me.

S: *Why is that so?*

L: The mothers are the givers of life, the nurturers, the teachers; to me my mother was everything. Mothers often have more compassion than the father does. And that is one of their biggest roles; it is to teach us to be kind to one another. Kindness is one of the most valuable lessons to learn.

S: *Tell me about that.*

L: My mother used to tell me that one act of kindness causes a chain reaction of kindness that continues to give back in a great cycle. She would always remind me that small, kind decisions make big impacts.

S: *Is there anyone in your tribe besides your mother that teaches these things?*

L: Our elders. The elders have been here the longest and are valuable teachers; they teach us so that one day we might become the teacher. I knew that I was bound to be a good teacher one day because when I used to spend time near the rivers listening to the water, that is what the water told me.

S: *The water told you this? Tell me more about that.*

L: The Great Spirit of the Earth speaks loudly by the water.

S: *What does it say?*

L: The Great Spirit talked to me about all kinds of things and the trees whispered about the cosmos and how vast everything is. I loved spending time by that river and the deep loving nature of the Earth there. The sun would glint off the water and I could see the mountains in the distance and that was where I would ask questions about life, and I always got answers. The Great Spirit showed me how to stay calm and approach things rather than react, and it prepared me for things to come. Although it didn't tell me everything, the Great Spirit showed me that I would become the mediator, the communicator that I am. I would mediate, not only between tribes, but for our interactions with very strange looking people. The river showed me scenes, sometimes they were confusing, especially the ones of the future where I saw myself next to very large buildings made of stone.

S: *What did these buildings look like?*

L: They were very tall, and I felt very small compared to them. It's like being surrounded by trees, but instead they are big and square.

S: *What were your houses like compared to these big buildings that you had never seen?*

L: Our houses are wooden houses that have rounded off the edges at the ends. Certain shapes are important to us as we recognize that circles are sacred; they symbolize the continuation of life.

S: *What else does the river show you?*

L: It showed me traveling to a faraway place by boat. I saw for the first time in the river these very white looking people with white hair, something I'd never seen before. My skin is very different, it's like a deep caramel color. The people in the river were so pale looking that, at first, when I saw this, I wondered if these people were ok because they were so white that I could see some of their veins! But I see that in these futuristic scenes that I'm with Black Fox and we're trying to sign something important.

S: *What does the river show you doing?*

L: We are there to sign a treaty, or at least trying to get some kind of peace. They were trying to take our lands. It has been an issue.

S: *Ok, let's move to another time in that life as Aniwaya. What do you notice now?*

L: I am remembering my life now a little in the future when I'm about twelve or thirteen, and the White Men started coming into my village.

S: *What was that like?*

L: I never thought that anything like this would ever happen, and it was horrible, just horrible! These White Men burned everything. They didn't care.

S: *Tell me about that.*

L: I remember that there was so much screaming, crying and dust everywhere from the horses and I ran into the forest with my dog and my horse, and my bow on my back, trying to get away. My mom told me to run but I didn't want to. I wanted to be strong. I wanted to fight. But she said that somebody had to make it. I didn't want it to be me! I wanted it to be her. My mother was everything, everything to me. She said that I had to escape because I was young, and I had more years ahead of me and so it made more sense for me to survive. I had other siblings, but all of them were brutally murdered that day.

S: *Tell me more.*

L: There was so much fire and smoke everywhere! I remember hiding in the woods; I found a cave close to a stream where I stayed for quite some time by myself, but I wasn't completely alone because I had my horse and my wolf, the wolf that I was raised with. I don't think I would have made it without them. My wolf was the one who got me through this hard time. He would comfort me by putting his head on my shoulder. At night he would bring me his kills and look at me with these understanding loving eyes as he would drop them in my lap. We were so connected; he understood enough to know that I was too sad to hunt. For a while after my family was killed, he would bring the kills to me each night. One night he brought me a rabbit and I tried so hard not to cry but I couldn't hold back my tears and I couldn't look him in the eyes because I didn't want my wolf to think that I was ungrateful. It was so nice of my wolf, but rabbits reminded me of my mother. One day when I was little, my mother caught a rabbit and showed me how to skin it and she said that one day I'd be a man and would show my child how to do the same. It was so hard to skin the rabbit alone, knowing that my mother was really gone, and it just reminded me of the horrible slaughter that happened to my beloved tribe. I had to eat though,

7

I knew that I had to use whatever I had at that time, and that this was a gift from the Creator, even if I didn't see it as one.

S: *Were you the only survivor, or did anyone else from your tribe make it out?*

L: My best friend Black Fox made it out as well, but we didn't see each other for a long time after. He had gotten injured while fighting the White Men and ran to a neighboring village. That tribe took him in even though he was an outsider. Each tribe is very similar, yet some of their ways vary from one another.

S: *Were their ways a lot different than your tribe's ways?*

L: A little, not drastically, some of their dances and ways of growing things were different so he had to relearn a few things, but he did bring our tribal knowledge to that tribe as well, and they were able to combine our tribal information with theirs and that helped their tribe become more prosperous. Because of this, Black Fox became very highly regarded.

S: *What about you? What happened after you hid in the forest? Did you see what happened to your village?*

L: I eventually went back and there was nothing! Just bodies and debris everywhere. I felt helpless and in shock. I was barely yet a man, but I was supposed to protect my tribe, and yet, here I was. I hadn't protected anyone. I felt like a failure and a failure to my name Aniwaya, the Great Wolf. People in my tribe always used to call me Wolf… when I still had a tribe.

S: *Why did you get that name? Was there a reason why that name was chosen for you?*

L: There was, and I received this right before the White Man came. It's a tradition within our tribe that everyone receives their name when they are around twelve or thirteen on a vision quest. They go up into the mountain by themselves until they receive their gift and their name. When I went, I stayed there for several days before anything happened. I was frustrated after the second day and hungry because it was important to fast until you received the messages. During the day I went to the water and continued

8

to wait, and at night I slept under the stars on the mountain. It was on the third night that I looked up into the sky, and at first, I saw three twinkling lights that morphed into shapes, and then finally, I saw it. I saw the shape of a white wolf and that is how I received my name. The white wolf said to me that my gift was leadership, even though I didn't want to lead, and I didn't understand what that meant at the time.

S: *What happened after you escaped the destruction of your village?*

L: I lived many years in the woods by myself with great sadness until I went into town one day and heard that there was more unrest with the White Man coming to take more lands. It was then that I knew I needed to get myself out of this sadness and do something. I knew that I needed to help. I had started to go into the town on a few occasions, and I spoke with an English-speaking man while I was there. It was a small town that was easy to ride into from the forest. But as I was talking to this man, he said something about the White Man's religions and that they were now killing just for religious reasons. This was all I could really understand from that townsman. It was hard for me with all of the different sounds of his language to understand everything that he was saying because I didn't speak English very well. It was in that moment of trying to decipher this man's difficult language that I decided if I was to help my people, then I would learn this language for them! The river had already shown me this when I was younger. It was just very hard to learn English at first, and there was a time when I almost gave up, but eventually I learned, even though throughout my whole life my accent was very strong.

S: *How did you learn English?*

L: I learned by going into town every day and speaking with the people there. Some of the people were not very nice, and English was very hard and different from my language. Their syllables are letters, and it was so different and confusing especially because our syllables are more sound based.

S: *Could you say a word in your language?*

L: My mother would call me "oosti", and it means little one. And "dinahey" means come here. That's the last word that my mother yelled right before…(Les started crying) right before we saw the White Men coming towards our village. My mother knew when she saw the smoke off in the distance that something terrible was about to happen. I will never forget that look that she had on her face. Somehow, she knew. We were the only tribe for miles. We knew our lands and we knew that the people coming were newcomers. Throughout everything we tried to be kind. But they did not accept our kindness; they continued to call us savages.

S: *That's what they called you? They called you savages?*

L: Yes, I found out later that they called us savages because of our dances and how we had clothes made of animal skin and feathers that we kept in our hair. We always tried to tell them that this was just our way of life, but they wouldn't accept that excuse. They thought we were crazy for thanking the animals that we ate or for honoring the Earth. They didn't understand why we considered everything a blessing. They didn't understand our ways. They said we were barbaric.

S: *Did they say that to you before they burned your village? Or no?*

L: When they burned our village the only word that I understood at that time was "savages." They always repeated that word as they themselves savagely took the scalps from our people's bodies. They somehow knew a lot about us because they understood that our hair was sacred to us. We always considered our hair to be our connection to the Earth and to Source. So not only were they scalping us to make our bodies look disgusting and mutilated, but they were trying to keep us from God. However, it changed nothing; we were and always are still connected regardless.

S: *Tell me more. What happened next after you learned English?*

L: When I learned English, I realized my higher purpose. I could be a mediator, just as the Great Spirit had once told me by the river. I could be a mediator for all of our tribes. Because now I had the tools to help when before I felt helpless. Learning English gave me a tool. Though my accent was still very strong, I was able to communicate, especially as I got older, with many different types of people. I even met darker skinned people, people with much darker skin than my own skin. And then I met people that were so pale they looked like the moon. And yet, I was able to communicate with all of them and with my people as well. And so, I understood my purpose in life, it was to be the bridge to help...to try to help stop what was to come.

S: *What came?*

L: We were forced out of our lands and made to walk.

When I brought Les back to full waking consciousness, she looked at me with surprise and a sense of recognition. It was the same look that many of my clients share when they understand things about their life that never made sense to them before. It's also a look of understanding that they are not just their physical body, that they have had other lifetimes in other times and the peace of knowing that there is truly no death. I asked Les if she had ever heard of Aniwaya before, and she said that she had! Les remembered that when she was little that she had had an imaginary friend named Aniwaya. But now it seemed as if this imaginary friend was not imaginary after all! Les claimed that her grandmother was Cherokee and that she was just as excited and curious as I to uncover more of Aniwaya's story.

CHAPTER 2:
FALLING IN LOVE IN THE EIGHTEEN HUNDREDS

There was obviously more that Aniwaya wanted to share so Les and I decided to work together again to find out more about Aniwaya's life. As I brought Les back into hypnosis, I told her to drift and float to where something important in Aniwaya's life was happening. Again, Aniwaya's voice surfaced and shared more about this tragic, yet fascinating life.

S: Ok. Let's move ahead in time to where something important is happening. What do you notice?

L: I remember falling in love with the most beautiful woman I'd ever met. She had the most beautiful soul, and she was very kind and funny and made lots of jokes that always made me laugh.

S: Tell me more about her.

L: She had dark straight hair and greenish eyes that were different from mine because mine were dark brown. Her eyes were so beautiful. I could see every color in her eyes as if they were internally ignited, like fire. Everything about her was absolutely beautiful, even the way that she always smelled like dried herbs and flowers. She reminded me of a flower. She was very kind and always gave more than she received. Even though she was from a neighboring tribe, she reminded me of my mother.

S: How did you meet her?

L: I met her after I had been living on my own for several years. When I started learning English in town and meeting more people, I curiously rode into the village where Black Fox lived, even though I didn't know that at the time. This village was very similar to the one I grew up in, although there were also many differences.

S: What happened when you rode into the village?

L: I guess I looked wild (Aniwaya laughed) because this beautiful woman came up to me, although (laugh) she almost looked sorry for me for some reason. I guess she thought I looked dirty, even though I did wash off in the river. Maybe I had a wild look in my eyes or maybe she saw that I was wild, or that I didn't have a home. I really don't know, but for whatever reason she felt compassion for me, and she gave me food. The tribal people there were so kind. They gave me new clothes, which was good because mine were falling apart. And I remember she sat next to me and brushed my hair. And that was the moment that I fell in love with her. I felt these intense feelings all throughout my body that I had never felt before when she started brushing my hair because hair is very sacred to us, it's our connection to the Great Spirit. Maybe it was a mixture of her kindness, her beauty, and her compassion, or maybe it was a combination of all of that that brought me instantly into a state of falling for her. I felt as if my body was on fire as she started to ask me questions about my life and about my family. I didn't want to, but I had to interrupt her to remind her that I couldn't talk about that while she was brushing my hair because feeling negative emotions while brushing your hair muddles the connection. So, I told her that she could ask me about other things. As we spoke there was something about her that was different. I had never felt this way before and I knew that I wanted her, to be around her more. When she started brushing my hair it felt as if with each movement of the brush I was falling deeper and deeper in love with her. I knew I loved her even if she didn't feel that way about me. I would do anything to be in her presence. I knew that I would do anything to win her heart.

S: What happened next?

L: I tried to think of something nice to do with her, so I started asking her to take night walks with me. It wasn't necessarily a walk; it was really just an excuse to be near her. We would look at the stars and she would tell me about the constellations, and I was amazed at how her tribe had said the same things that my tribe had said! Both of our tribes had said that we came from the three stars in the Big Dipper, that is what you call it now, but we called it the ladle. We called it the ladle because it was said that it would carry us into our new knowing. Someday the Star People will come down and scoop us up and take us with them.

S: *And it was the big three stars within the Big Dipper where you were from?*

L: Yes, but the night looked much different then because you could see all of the stars clearly.

S: *What else would you talk about on these night walks?*

L: We talked about the Creation Story. It's nice to look at the stars and talk about where we come from. I was surprised that there were only a few differences in our stories. Some of the differences I found very interesting. My tribe believed that there was this woman who they called the Star Woman. She was originally human but achieved enlightenment through spending a lot of time in nature and harmonizing herself with her environment. And because she was able to fully harmonize herself with nature, she was able to ascend into the heavens. And when she did, she went to the planet that had what we called the Tribe in the Sky. We understood that we had star ancestors and that we all came from the stars, but the story that my tribe told was that this Star Woman started to miss her human family. On this planet, there were different crops, and the story goes that when she picked a turnip, it left a large hole that she fell into, arriving back on Earth. She was said to have been impregnated by the Tribes in the Sky before she fell, and our tribe believed that when she fell through the hole, she fell through a portal. And my love's tribe said that she just fell and when she fell, she died, but that the two children that she was impregnated with from the Tribes in the Sky survived. The tribe I came from said that a flock of geese broke her fall, and she was able to land safely and get back to her family.

S: *How did you feel that these stories were so similar?*

14

L: It was interesting because like I said, we were separated by many miles. There was no way for us to know of other people having these stories. We never saw any outsiders or talked to anyone else other than the White Men who came to destroy our village. I felt that the fact that these stories were so similar shows that there must have been some truth to them. Even our stories about the first people and the first groups were the same.

S: *Could you tell me those stories?*

L: We believed that there were four groups of people that originated from the north, and they started from the top of the world and migrated out going in the different directions of the wind. The different directions were north, south, east, and west and they were all given different elements to guard. The northern people were given the element of fire because of the snow; they needed it to keep them warm. These people ended up having blond hair and blue eyes from being in the snow. And then there were the people of the south that were given the gift of water. These people were darker in skin color. The people of the east were of Asian descent, and they were given the gift of the wind. Because of this they could use breathing exercises when they were protecting themselves. And my tribe, our people were given the gift of the Earth. We could communicate with her in ways that the other tribes couldn't. Just like the other tribes could communicate with their elements in ways that we couldn't.

S: *How did you communicate with the Earth exactly?*

L: We would be still in nature and focus our breathing and energy inwards, and through that calibration we would be able to communicate with the Earth and recognize the signs the Earth would give us. Sometimes we would also use the sun to give us information.

S: *Could you tell me about that? How did you do that?*

L: We would sit in the sun and allow the sun to bring information and energy into our bodies. There is an instant feeling of connection while sitting in the sun. Just like the plants, we are hungry for the sun as well. We would imagine there being a straight connection between the sun and our heads, and then, we would take the sun's energy and continue bringing it down through our bodies and back into the Earth. It's a gift to be a channel for the sun and to send this energy into the Earth because it not only helps the Earth to do this, but it also helps you as well.

S: *Was this different or the same practice as your love's tribe?*

L: It was surprisingly the same! And her tribe believed that we originated from those first people as well and we all had a deep connection to the Earth. We all understood the Earth as a reflection of ourselves.

S: *What did your tribe think about the Star People?*

L: My tribe knew that the Star People were our ancestors.

S: *What did the Star People look like? Do you know?*

L: They looked similar to us, but they were very slender and had elongated faces. It was rare for us to meet with them, but we knew they were there. Their skin isn't blue but gives off a blue iridescent hue so you would see them as being blue, but that's just their energy. We called these people the Star People, or the Tribe in the Sky. We greatly appreciated them and trusted them because they gave us what we needed to survive. However, when we were visited by them or communicated with them, they always said that they weren't allowed to interfere too much. So, when we asked them if we should share our gifts with other people, like when the White Man first showed up, they couldn't make the decision for us. We were scared and we wanted to know what would happen. But they said that we would have to decide what we thought was right.

S: *Were you upset that the Star People didn't help you with the White Man? Were any of your people upset with this Tribe in the Sky?*

L: Of course, some were, but some understood that it really wasn't the White Man we were fighting with. We understood the concept of a negative force that had taken over most of the White Man and we also understood that there are always boundaries and with every hardship there is beauty in it. Even though it was terrible what ended up happening, we found that through it all we were always guided and that we are still strong and resilient.

S: *Is there anything else that you and the woman you loved would talk about on these night walks?*

L: We talked about the Moon Eyed people, because in both of our tribes there were many stories and legends about them. Some people thought that they were just White Men and some people thought that they were a hybrid of some sort. Some people thought that they could be from the Tribe in the Sky or the Star People and that they are called Moon Eyes because the sunlight is too harsh for them and it's hard for their lighter eyes to see. Some believed that they were more active at night because they could communicate with the moon.

S: *What did you and your love believe?*

L: We thought that they were actually just the light eyed Indians, but that they were seers. The Great Spirit by the river had told me that it was a genetic mark of communication that they could tap into. It's like a different radio frequency and it shows up on the gene. It's a recessive gene, and it shows up as blue eyes. And so, it's hard to pass on, but it's usually passed between mother and child, not from the father.

S: *Why is that and do all indigenous people born with blue eyes have this?*

L: They do. Just like with the matriarchal traditions that have followed us from our ancient culture, information and those genes are carried on from the mother.

S: *Where did the light eyed Indians originate?*

L: If I look at my life from a higher perspective, I can answer questions about this a little better if you have questions. I can see that they did come from the Tribe in the Sky. They are human hybrids, so part human, part Star Person.

S: *Where did the Star People come from?*

L: Some came from a planet that looks blue and there is another one that looks pink, but this blue one is a place of seven suns and seven moons. There are creatures that roam that planet that look almost like big, long eels and some look like manta rays. There are people that look like people, but their face isn't as wide as mine and their skin is much lighter. They have very light hair and very light eyes, and they are who we get the green eyes from. It's the combination of their blue eyes and our brown eyes that creates the green eyes with yellow specs that the woman I fell in love with has.

S: *Why did they come to Earth?*

L: There are many opportunities on Earth, many resources and there are many beings from many different planets who have come to Earth to not only experience all that Earth has to offer, but also to help. There are many here to help the Earth and the consciousness of the planet. However, it is known to us that they can't interfere too much.

S: *How far away was your tribe and your love's tribe from one another?*

L: Many miles and many mountains in between. I'm trying to see it on a map, or where it would be considered now. I think she was somewhere in Georgia or South Carolina, and I was from Alabama, on the Tennessee border. So, where my old tribe was located and where this tribe was located were very far apart, they were many miles from one another.

S: *What else did you talk about on your night walks?*

L: We took many walks; we would walk and talk about all of the stories that we grew up hearing. I told her what I could remember about the story of the first strawberry. It was a story that I remembered hearing as a child and there were parts that I forgot.

S: *Tell me the story of the first strawberry?*

L: It was a story about a tribal woman who was picking berries one day and she wanted her husband to help her pick the berries as well, but he said he was busy. And so, this woman got so upset that she ran away. The man, in his regret of not helping his wife, prayed to have a gift of some kind, something that she would love, the gift of a sweet berry to give her. And so, the husband ran after her while looking for any type of delicious looking berry that he could find, and on the way there he found this bush of what you call strawberries. He had never seen them before! He grabbed some and when he gave them to the woman, they were so delicious that she forgave him at once! And that was the story of the first strawberry!

S: *What happened when you told this story to the woman you were in love with?*

L: (Les laughed) She frowned at me at first and then burst out laughing so hard because she thought it was the funniest story. She said it was completely unrealistic! She said that there was no way a woman, a Cherokee woman, would just run away after such a small argument and then come back over a strawberry! She laughed and laughed and said she wasn't falling for it, and she jokingly punched me in the arm. Her laughter and touch were always so powerful to me it sent electricity all throughout my body. I was so in love; I would do anything to win her heart. But I didn't tell her, I couldn't tell her how I felt! I felt insecure around her. How could someone like her possibly want me too. Maybe she just spent time with me because she felt sorry for me! I didn't have the courage to tell her my feelings. I was so in love with her that it scared me deeply that she might not feel the same. Even when we weren't together, I thought about her every second of my day. Saying goodbye to her before I went to England was so hard. I told myself that I would tell her how I felt, but I failed and left without telling her.

S: *Why did you have to go to England?*

L: Since I was the mediator for our tribe I was volunteered to go. We were told that some of us needed to go to England to discuss and sign a treaty so that we could keep our lands, but it was all a lie.

It seems there are so many of us with deep memories of our past lives in indigenous cultures all around the world. As I was uncovering Les's past life memories as Aniwaya another client regressed to a similar lifetime. This is

Penelope's session.

S: *What do you become aware of?*

P: There are little bushes growing out of rocks as I'm walking down to a very deep pool of water. I just want to bathe in the water, but I just sit by the edge and put my feet in. I know that I could get in trouble for putting my feet in or bathing in this water, so I keep looking around to make sure no one is coming.

S: *Why can't you bathe in this water?*

P: This is our drinking reservoir and it's forbidden.

S: *Tell me about yourself, can you describe yourself?*

P: I'm a child, no more than about eight years old. I have very soft moccasins on my feet and the same type of beads hanging down the animal skin I'm wearing on the lower half as I have on the upper half of my body. The rocks are hard and hot and so it's a relief to put my moccasins back on.

S: *Where do you live in this place?*

P: I live with a tribe in a village. The people are dark with long hair, some of us have feathers in our hair, but I just have a headband to keep my hair off my face.

S: *What about your home?*

P: There are other children that I share a room with, but they are smaller than I am, and I'm supposed to be watching them. Most of the day I spend grinding some sort of grain on a flat stone that grinds the grain into patties that we then put into the oven. It's constant work because we have a lot of mouths to feed. It's time consuming, but I prefer this to scrapping hides. I hate scrapping hides; it's my least favorite job. That is tedious hard work to get the hair off the hide!

S: *What is your life like there?*

P: It's busy but very peaceful, quiet, compassionate. I enjoy this place even though I'm busy.

S: *What else do you notice there?*

P: The pottery is beautiful and making pottery is what I love to do. We make it into all different colors and many different shapes. You have to work the dough to make it soft and then you can shape it into different things. I make little dolls for some of the children that I live with, and I've made some of the beads that I'm wearing.

S: *Ok, let's leave that scene. What do you notice next?*

P: Something is happening because there is a lot of screaming. I don't know what happened, I'm looking down at my body from above.

S: *Now that you've left your body can you see from a different perspective what happened?*

P: Yes, I was killed instantly by a blow to the back of my head. A large group of White Men came and burnt down our village and destroyed everything with it.

CHAPTER 3:
GOING TO ENGLAND

I was curious to find out more about Aniwaya's trip to England and what that was like for a Native American to go there in those days.

S: *Tell me more about your trip to England. How did you get there?*

L: The boat we took was not like any of our canoes. It was a big boat, and a very long journey. I was lucky that I was used to being on the water, but even so, there were many, many storms along the way, and we weren't even sure if we were going to make it. I think in a sense we knew that this was not going to be an easy trip, and that it might not end the way we wanted it to.

S: *Who did you travel with?*

L: I was traveling with Black Fox, who was also sent out on this mission.

S: When you were on the ship and going to England, how long did it take you to get there?

L: It was many moons, it felt like forever. I didn't think we were ever going to make it because there was no land on any sides of the ship for so long! And I didn't understand how they navigated because it was so different. They used the stars at night, but they also used something that they called a compass during the day and we just…we could still see the stars during the day, but these people couldn't.

S: *Why is that?*

L: They weren't open enough like we were. If you are willing to see, then you will, but if you're not willing to see, you can't, and it was that simple.

S: *How did you navigate?*

L: We used the stars to navigate, but we also had a very strong intuition and internal guidance system that we used that these people didn't have for some reason. Their energy was different than ours. Sometimes on the ship it was even harder for us to connect with the spirit of the ocean because the men on board had an energy that almost acted like a fog that we would have to disperse in order to make our connections.

S: *What was it like when you finally arrived in England? What did you notice?*

L: We must've arrived while I was still sleeping because I remember waking up to a lot of yelling and the sounds of the boat creaking as people were hitching the ropes to the port. As Black Fox and I walked off the boat, people started staring at us, and to us it looked like we had stepped into a completely different world.

S: *What did you notice?*

L: It was so crowded! That was the first thing that we noticed. There were so many buildings built right next to other buildings made of stones that were uneven but were stuck together. They were also so tall, much taller than the buildings that we have. I had seen this before in the river when I was young, but it was nothing like seeing it in person. It was overwhelming.

S: *Tell me more.*

L: Everywhere you looked there were many wooden signs, armories, and places of work for people, and there were many people in the streets. The streets were so tight that there was only enough room for one carriage to go through at a time in most places. It looked as if the people just lived on top of one other.

S: *What did the buildings look like?*

L: The buildings were strange and were made with many different colors. Some had red stones, some with grey stones, whitish stones and then some with all of these different color variations at once. And they have roofs that have what looks almost looks like stones overlapping each other instead of wood like we have. The shapes of these buildings were square, which was strange since we understood the importance of having certain angles or rounded edges.

S: *Tell me about that.*

L: When one has rounded edges then the energy works in a circular shape and spiraling motion. Certain shapes help for healing as well, like the teepee shape, as it allows the energy to move in a circular motion up to a point. However square shapes are not conducive to healing. Square shapes do not concentrate power. Rounded shaped dwellings like a cave or our houses are considered places of power. I wonder why these people do not understand this. But what I notice the most about this place is the smell! The smell is horrible!

S: *What does it smell like there?*

L: It smells absolutely disgusting! People just throw their waste and their dirty bath water in the street! And the carriages that go by let their horses defecate in the streets and they don't clean it. And because this is not an environment that seems balanced there doesn't appear to be any animals that would naturally come and clean that up, or a layer of earth that would naturally turn it into dirt. Instead, there is a layer of stone in between the people and the earth.

S: *What do the people look like?*

L: The people look dirty and worn as if they work really hard all day. They have these barrels that they wash in, almost like a bucket. It looks like they wash in it and then they dump the bucket out into the street instead of just bathing in a river that's already running. It makes no sense. But the people look very different than we do.

S: *How are they different?*

L: They have very pale, white skin, but they don't look as different as they think we look!

S: *What type of clothes are they wearing?*

L: A lot of the women are wearing white aprons on muted colored dresses that have white collars. The people just seem so busy, almost like they forget to take a moment and breathe in some air. I hardly see any men in this city because they are sent to work elsewhere. Most of the people we see in town are women because they are the ones who are cleaning up their houses, taking care of children, and giving them baths while the men go to work. It looks like most of the men in the city work for the city, like the bank and the council and things like that. It appears as if everyone here wants esteemed jobs that allow for one person to look better than the other.

S: *What happened after you got there? Where did they bring you?*

L: When we got there, we went immediately to the council house. No one brought us there and it was hard to find because it was hard for us to navigate the city. It was confusing and loud, and the noises were overwhelming, but we finally found the place. We figured that we were in the right place when we saw men with white wigs calling us over and it was obvious to them that we were the people that they were waiting on. They were not very friendly, they seemed to feel as if it was their job to preach to us, scold us, and tell us that what we practiced was witchcraft.

S: *Why?*

L: They told us that speaking to anything other than what they deemed of as God is devil worshiping and a sin. I'm not sure why they put a limit on God? How do they know what God is versus something else? It doesn't make sense. And so, I try to explain to them some of our ways and why we do the things that we do. Not only do they seem extremely offended by everything that I say, but they continue to ridicule and preach to me.

S: *So, they call it witchcraft?*

L: Yes, that's what they call it. They say that lesser men have been hanged for believing the things that we do. And I say that I am no lesser man, I am just an equal man. I explain to them that we are all the same, every man, woman and child is equal I tell them, and they get even more offended when I say that.

S: *What happens next?*

L: We sat for a long time trying to get what we were told was a treaty, signed. But it seems like they never intended to agree or to sign anything in the first place. They appear to just want to lecture us and ridicule us. We have done everything that they have asked us to do. I thought the whole point of a treaty was for both sides to agree and come together on this. And it just seems like they just don't care. They act like they have somewhere better to be, as if we aren't worth anything and that we didn't travel across the big water to get here. We risked our lives to get here!

S: *So, all they had to say was that you were practicing witchcraft? So, what happened?*

L: There was one person, only one, who came and tried to help us. He was a White Man, but he understood more about us than the others and he tried to vouch for us. But since he was only one and there were many people against us, he was outvoted. I remember he ended up losing his position over this. He was even beaten and asked to leave the city. They said that when he stood up for us, he showed his true colors.

S: *What happened after that?*

L: We were not welcome anywhere and we ended up finding a wooded area outside of the city and just tried to live off the land while we waited for something to happen. But the issue with that was that people claimed to own all of the land! It was so strange and did not make sense. How can anyone say that they own land when it's the Earth's land? Nothing here made sense.

S: *Tell me more.*

L: These people had so many strange and different traditions that we just couldn't understand. One of the strangest things was that they used coins as a form of payment instead of trade. This was so different from our traditions. In our tribe we understood that there was power and energy that is exchanged when someone gives a gift. And that is why whenever you look at a gift from someone, you think of that person. There is an energetic imprint that is left on that item that surpasses time.

S: What happened next?

L: I just wanted to go home; I wanted to be with the woman I loved. I told myself that when I saw her next, I would finally tell her that I loved her. Nothing was going to work here, and Black Fox and I decided to just go home. It was obvious that coming here had been a waste of time and that we were never going to be able to come to any agreement. I felt like we were there forever, and no one except that one man wanted to listen to us.

S: How long were you there?

L: It was several moons, maybe longer. We went back to the council house every day trying to get someone to listen to us.

S: Did you ever sign anything?

L: No, maybe others did at some point, but we never signed the treaty we were supposed to sign. It was all a lie.

S: What happened next?

L: It took us a long time to get back home, many, many moons.

S: When you got home, was the woman that you loved there?

L: Yes, and on the whole journey home I was worried. I was worried that she would've forgotten about me, or that something could've happened to her while I was away. I couldn't bear the thought, so to handle my feelings I wrote her love letters that I never sent. Later on in my life I showed her some of these letters and she laughed at the fancy ink saying that I would be getting a big head because I used such fancy black ink. But I never did, I never did like the English ways, I liked our ways of doing things. Our ways made more sense to me. But all the experiences in England weren't bad. We did meet some interesting people, but all in all I never wanted to go back.

CHAPTER 4:
THE LITTLE PEOPLE

The Trail of Tears has many untold stories unlike anything I have ever read in books. Here are more of Aniwaya's memories.

S: *What was it like when you got back home to your tribe?*

L: When I arrived back, I didn't see the woman I loved anywhere. My stomach sank and I thought of all the possibilities that could've happened. But my anxiety quickly went away as I heard from a villager that she was just out picking berries.

S: *What happened when you saw her?*

L: I didn't see her approach me when she got back; she startled me by throwing her arms around me with excitement and her hands were still stained with blackberries. Her beautiful eyes that always looked like the universe were so beautiful and mesmerizing that I froze. I couldn't say anything, I just stared at her and regrettably, I didn't tell her I loved her.

S: *What happened next?*

L: We didn't settle in for very long. Even though Black Fox and I had had such a long journey, there was a lot of unrest within the tribe. There was talk that we needed to leave, that the White Men were approaching, and we needed to figure out what to do next.

S: *Could you tell me when the Trail started? What happened? Did they come and tell you to leave by force? What was it like when they first made you start walking?*

L: It was obvious that they wanted an excuse to take our lands, and going to England, although exhausting and challenging, wasn't enough. They hated us. There were even more attacks on our tribe while I was gone. And we decided that there would be no real way to have peace with this constant threat. We had lost so many people already, there was too much at stake to stay. So, for the sake of our nation, we ultimately decided to walk the Trail instead of fighting.

S: *Tell me more about this.*

L: **There was word that the Nunnehi, the Little People, had come to our tribe to warn us. They said that a terrible tragedy was about to happen to our people and that if we wanted, they would take us to a safe place within the mountains where we would be safe. Many tribes were told to pack up enough belongings and to be prepared to leave in seven days if they wished to go with them.**

S: *Did anyone go with them?*

L: Yes. The tribal people that did go with the Little People went underground deep within the mountains. I remember playing by one of the entrances to the underground caves in the mountains. There was a large stone that was rolled away, and it revealed the entrance into these mountains. According to our legends, those who went into the tunnels are still there or have ascended into a different dimension. That was their choice.

S: *What do you mean when you say Little People; who are the Little People?*

L: The Little People are just beings living in and out of our dimension. We, the native people, have a relationship with the Little People because we are kind and respect the Earth and the Little People help those who do the same, and so, at times, they've helped us. But they also have cultural differences amongst themselves just as humans do. And there are many different types.

S: *Why do they come in and out of the dimensions?*

L: Sometimes they come into this dimension just for supplies or to be of service. They are very sentient and go in and out of many dimensions.

S: *Do they eat food and wear clothes as well?*

L: Yes. The ones that I'm talking about wore clothes similar to us and even made tiny beads as well. They need sustenance just as any being who wishes to stay in this realm does. Without food or sustenance, the body fades and becomes spirit again in this dimension. They would be hard for you to see as they can go in and out of this dimension at will.

S: *Is this similar to Sasquatch?*

L: Yes. The Sasquatch comes in and out of this dimension looking for berries and supplies, things like that. The Sasquatch are very sentient creatures as well and are the guardians of the forests and that is why we often see them.

S: *Tell me more about them? How do they travel in and out of dimensions?*

L: They have what you would refer to as an entirely freed pineal gland and perfectly firing nerve connections to sense the air and energy around them while they use thought to come in and out of our dimension. They are more native to the Earth than humans are. And they travel in and out of dimensions within this Earth as humans do as well. Humans just aren't aware of it.

S: *Humans do as well?*

L: Yes, all the time. You may not be aware that you travel in and out of this dimension during your dream state. And every moment on this Earth is like a picture that exists forever and becomes part of the time dimension that we can travel back to in order to collect and find our missing soul pieces and story. Every step we take we move through time and therefore we move through dimensions. This is an ever-evolving process.

I had never heard about the Little People before until I took a trip to Utah and visited a ranch known by the name of Blind Frog Ranch. On the ranch in a cave were very tiny beads said to be from the Little People. What struck me as odd was the fact that they were buried under the sand and were so small it didn't make sense that a full-sized human hand had created them. Perhaps what Aniwaya said was true that the Little People live among us without us being aware.

S: *Were you able to get your belongings or did they just force you out onto the Trail all of a sudden?*

L: No. It was extremely violent. They came by force. Some of the tribe was taken and forced into camps. But for those of us still there, and who did not go with the Nunnehi, we grabbed what little we could because they didn't give us any time. It was either we fight, or we walk.

S: *Why didn't you go with the Nunnehi?*

L: We knew our mission was to walk. If we all left, or even if we all died, then our legacy would only be in the astral plane and in order to keep a written and oral record, we needed to walk to preserve what we could. We felt we had a duty and a mission to the preservation of our information.

S: *What did you take with you?*

L: We grabbed only what we could carry on our backs. In the little time we had to prepare, we put things in blankets and tied them together with little strips of leather. And that was how we carried what little belongings we had. We were able to take only a few of our horses and put a few things on them as well. The whole thing was heartbreaking, devastating. I always knew that I would be protected because I always had my wolf and my mother in spirit with me as a protector. But this also made things difficult because we were all treated so terribly that I had to communicate telepathically with my wolf to stop him from attacking the horrible guards. There were several times that I had to stop him from killing the man with the mustache.

S: *Who was the man with the mustache?*

L: The man with the mustache was one of the guards who came to force us off our lands. He was full of hate for us and seemed to hate me the most. He had a large scar over his left eye and brown greasy hair. Not only did he ooze with hate for me, but he hated us all terribly. He rode the Trail on horseback and loved to be the cause of our pain, and he found great pleasure in our torture. He often kicked our people, sometimes even fatally while we walked. And each time he approached one of us, I would have to call my wolf and remind him to stay calm because I didn't want my wolf to attack him and then be killed in the process. We were surrounded. The guards on horseback also had ammunition and we didn't. They had bullets made of silver. I was constantly afraid that my wolf would attack one of them and that it would cause them to kill us all because they thought we weren't worth anything anyway. They thought that they would be doing the world a favor by getting rid of us. I know that the memory of this man has shown up in Les's dreams, but now she can finally understand who this person is.

S: *Why does he show up in her dreams? Can you tell me more about the man with the mustache? Did you see him a lot on the Trail?*

L: He was absolutely horrible. He stayed around my area a lot. The problem was that he saw himself in me. We were roughly the same age, about the same height and the only real difference was that we came from two completely different backgrounds. He had lost his parents early on too, just as I had, and I tried so hard to get him to understand how similar we were, but he saw my kindness as a weakness. He saw the compassion that I possessed and how I took care of my people, and this made him so angry. He was angry at the universe, at God, because no one had ever taken care of him that way. My very presence bothered him. I remember that he oozed anger, almost like a vapor; the anger radiated off of him. If he was upset or if something frustrated him, he would often take it out on me. Sometimes he tied me up and that is where he would flog me over and over again trying to make me break so that he could feel satisfied, so that maybe he wouldn't feel so much pain inside. But to his dismay, no matter what he did to me, his pain would never leave.

CHAPTER 5: THE ANCESTORS

Many stories talk about the wisdom of the ancestors. As I worked with Les to uncover more of Aniwaya's memories, interesting information from his ancestors surfaced.

S: *What was it like to walk the Trail of Tears?*

L: It was a testament to our spirit; it pushed us all to the edge. Many didn't survive. The mountains and the terrain were difficult to walk on by foot. Most of our animals were killed. We were brutally pushed on by many angry sweaty and dirty looking men. Our people weren't allowed to take many of their belongings. None of their tools, only what they could carry in their arms or on their backs. So, some people took blankets, even if it was hot, because they knew they would be walking for months, and they wouldn't survive the cold without something to keep them warm. And the White Men were mean, corralling us like cattle, as if we didn't matter. It was amazing to us all that they didn't even care about our children, as if we weren't even humans like them.

S: *What did these people pushing you look like?*

L: They looked dirty and unkempt. I bet they never walked a mile in their life. And here we were, walking hundreds of miles and yet our feet still stood. However, as things got harder for us and as I felt myself get close to my own breaking point, my mother's support and communication with me grew stronger.

S: *Tell me about that.*

L: She would talk with me while I walked. She wanted me to survive so she would comfort me and tell me all about what she was doing on the other side, and that she was safe, and that she needed me to make it. I think she kept telling me that she was safe so that I didn't worry about how her transition into the afterlife was.

S: *What was her transition like?*

L: It was abrupt. She was confused at first, and it was hard for her to let go because I was still there, and she knew how sad I was. She didn't transition for a while because she wanted to ease my grief and she told me later that she had been with me every day when I lived alone in the forest. It took her a while to trust and go back to where all souls go. I'm not sure exactly where that is but it looks like the sun. But after she transitioned back to oneness, she had more awareness and strength and our communication got even clearer.

S: *Tell me about that.*

L: As I walked, my mother became a catalyst for our ancestors to channel wisdom and patience through me, which was a very hard thing for me to learn in this life. My ancestors would tell me that I had to learn to be patient, and forgive the people who hated me, even though they hated me for no reason.

S: *Where did your mother go when she returned to oneness?*

L: She described it like a big white beam of light that took her to this place. It's the same place I've seen the animals go when they leave their bodies. There is a guiding line of light so that you know where to go. And when my mother died, she was fighting against that pull so hard, like a mama bear with a cub.

S: *When she arrived there, she was still able to communicate with you?*

L: Yes, she was able to communicate with me better than when she was Earth-bound. However, I had to adjust my frequency to be able to talk to her and the ancestors. They had a higher frequency once they went into the beam of light. But I couldn't just talk to anyone. It had to be people that I had interactions with, or my ancestors. There is coding in the DNA that allowed me to only connect with MY ancestors. I couldn't connect with other tribes' ancestors.

S: *How did you change your frequency? Was there a practice that you used? What did you do to do that?*

L: Almost like the way I contact you through Les. I would focus on making my body as still as possible first and I would tune into the Earth by putting my feet on the ground and sending my energy to the center of the Earth so that the Earth could send me energy back in a continuous loop. It's a continuous cycle. And through that I was able to adjust to the frequency that was needed for me to communicate.

S: *So, by communicating and doing that loop with the Earth, you could get into the right frequency?*

L: Yes, it's actually a very easy and underutilized tool, but through this I was able to communicate with ancestors, chiefs, and other Star People that I had never met before in this lifetime. Some of the ancestors were from ancient lifetimes so long before mine that it was harder for me to learn to trust them at first. But I eventually did and talking to the ancestors was how I made it through such horror.

S: *What did the ancestors say to you?*

L: I had so many questions as we walked, and they would answer. It gave me something to look forward to. It gave me hope as I walked the Trail. It took me out of thinking about utter despair and I was so grateful to be able to talk to them.

S: *What did you ask them?*

L: I wanted to know more about our history. I wanted to understand more about what was happening, and what they told me was nothing like anything I had ever heard before.

S: *What did they say?*

L: **They said that our tribes were very special and that we were from two ancient places, but one in particular was where our sacred culture and knowledge came from.** It was a beautiful society on a beautiful island. People were full of compassion for one another, and they used certain crystals there to communicate with their ancestors. It was a matriarchal society like ours and knowledge was passed down from mother to daughter just like in our tribes.

S: *What was this island like?*

L: This island must've been very special because whenever the ancient ancestors talked about it there was melancholy feeling in the fact that it no longer existed. When it did exist, it was a beautiful island full of beautiful flowers and plants. And my people carry, not only the traditions, but our knowledge about many things from this place. Sometimes as the ancestors described this island to me, I could vaguely remember my own memories of this place. My people, although we looked different then, lived there. The ancestors described how this island sank many moons ago and my people are the direct descendants of the survivors from this beautiful continent. However, we are also descendants of another ancient island which was destroyed as well.

S: *Do you know what these places are called?*

L: I do not have a name for these places. We used to call them the Lands Before, but if I search Les's vocabulary the beautiful island would be called what is known as Lemuria. The other Land Before was what you would call Atlantis.

When Les said this, I remembered that when Jen and I were working on my book "A Hypnotist's Journey to Atlantis" I had her draw the symbol of Lemuria while she was still deep under hypnosis, and I was surprised that it was the same as the symbol the Native Americans and other indigenous cultures use.

S: *Was the symbol of the Land Before the same symbol that you use now?*

36

L: Yes, it is. **It is the Four Directions symbol that contains sacred information. This sacred symbol is a carrier of this consciousness. The symbol itself is able to send information or conjure information based on intention.** Our tribes have agreed to be the keepers of this symbol and the keepers of the sacred knowledge. Our native cultures are some of the most powerful on the Earth and our ancient powers are still with us.

S: *Where do the symbols come from?*

L: They all originate from the Star People. The Star People used these symbols to teach us many things. The Four Corners symbol has many meanings, but one is the representation of our origins coming from one sacred point moving out into four different directions, only to return once again, and return to oneness.

S: *Could you tell me more about the other Land Before, the place we call Atlantis?*

L: The ancestors described the experiments that had happened in that place you call Atlantis and that we had DNA from the survivors of this place as well. Some of these people that were affected by the experiments were very powerful and special, yet they were different looking and so were looked down upon by one society but understood by ours. We understood them, and they integrated within our culture. Some of our shape shifting and animalistic abilities come from these survivors of that ancient place. These survivors from Atlantis and Lemuria integrated into our native cultures and spread out all throughout the world and many of our symbols and drawings come from this time.

S: *Could you tell me more about what the ancestors say about the Star People?*

L: They explained that time does not exist and everything that has ever happened or has happened is also happening now. They explain that many of the Star People are different versions of us, sometimes even in the future, depending on what path is taken. These Star People, although fully living in their time and space, are really humans who have evolved in different ways. Some of these Star People that would appear as grey have lost their planet, their emotions, and have had to live on ships within the cosmos, and some of these Star People who appear blueish and almost purple have advanced so much in their spirituality that they have become enlightened. Like I said, some of these Star People are just us in the future, although they could also be considered our past as well as time is not relevant.

S: *Tell me more.*

L: The Star People have passed knowledge throughout cultures, and it is knowledge that we still carry, like the knowledge about the circle and the four directions.

S: *What does the circle mean?*

L: All symbols that come from the Star People can change meaning depending on the energy and intention placed upon them, so the circle can mean different things. However, many times it means the continuation of this never-ending life and experiment. The circle with a dot in the middle is a powerful symbol often used by the Star People to remind you of your point of perspective within your sphere of perception.

As Les said this, it was interesting to me because many of my clients who have experienced extra-terrestrial contact and have remembered going on board their ships, often see the light at the bottom of the ship in the shape of a circle with a dot in the middle.

L: These symbols are often shown to us because they are in our ancient genetic memories and are meant to stimulate these memories, so they become ingrained in us. Those who don't have past lives on Earth are taught using these symbols in their visitations by the Star People. Time is irrelevant when it comes to symbols, and they are holographic in that they have many meanings enfolded into them. These symbols are tools; they are coded. The symbols connect us all together. If you take the circle and cross and you add another smaller inner ring, then it is another symbol for what you would call Atlantis, and If you add another outer ring then it is the symbol for creating our next evolutionary experience.

CHAPTER 6:
THE SURVIVORS FROM THE LAND BEFORE

I wanted to find out more about the connection between the natives and the survivors of Lemuria, so I had another session with Les.

S: *Can you tell me more about the survivors of that ancient island where the Four Corners symbol comes from? The island of Lemuria?*

L: Our culture still carries on these traditions through our stories and even our dances that point back to these ancient places. By keeping this knowledge through stories, the message was never found by the wrong people. **The only way for messages to make it through time is to code them and keep the story veiled in a way that keeps it common enough to not be worshiped but rare enough to be kept in our archives for study.**

S: Tell me more.

L: From what the ancestors show me, they want me to start from the beginning before the other Star People and other colonizers came to Earth. In the beginning, the Earth planet was inhabited by beings that looked very reptile-like until giant humanoid Star People came to the planet and forced these reptile-like beings underground within the tunnel systems in the Earth.

S: The tunnel systems are that old?

L: Yes, and when these giant Star People changed the original humans into more advanced humans, splicing their genes and giving them upgrades in their DNA, they evolved because of the interference from the Star People.

However, the intention behind these genetic upgrades from these giant Star People was to make humans into slaves. That was their original plan.

S: *Why did these large Star People want to create human slaves and why did they come to Earth?*

L: To mine gold as it was a valuable resource to them. But this element was dwindling on their planet and Earth was abundant in this resource.

S: *Tell me more.*

L: Over the years as humans evolved, these large Star People started to procreate with the human species and became what was known as your demigods. They were very large, giant-like.

S: *What happened to the reptile-like beings?*

L: These large Star People advanced these reptilian-like beings in return for the promise that the reptile beings would not interfere with the humans.

S: *So, what happened to the large Star People who were enslaving the humans?*

L: Other Star beings from all over the galaxy became aware of what was happening to the humans and intervened on behalf of the humans, forcing these giant Star People out. However, during this time there was an unexpected energy that found its way to the planet. This was a negative energy; some would call this the Fear virus. However, upsetting to the experiment, it gave more challenges and depth to the human experience.

S: *Do you know what happened to the island that used the Four Corners symbol? The beautiful island? Lemuria?*

L: It was destroyed, torn apart, and sunk to the bottom of the ocean.

S: *So how did your tribes get to America?*

L: Many of us were brought over by boat.

S: *Why the Americas?*

L: **When the Land Before (Atlantis) was destroyed the energetic grid lines under the Earth shifted so the energetic power point on Earth moved**

from this ancient, advanced island (Atlantis) to the Americas. There were strong points on the Earth's grid that were stronger than others and this strong energetic power point that was once under this ancient, advanced island (Atlantis) shifted to allow that area to heal. And so, many of the indigenous cultures from the Land Before (Lemuria) were instructed to move to these lands here (America) because America would be the stage for the transition times we are in now. Of course, some moved to other places around the world and kept the sacred (Lemurian) traditions there as well.

S: *Tell me more. How did these energetic points shift?*

L: The human body and the Earth represent one another, and just as the brain has energetic grids that may shift, so does the Earth. And after the destruction of Atlantis, the most powerful zone for the shift went from Atlantis to North America. Many native Lemurians were taken by boat to the Americas to be the holders of knowledge and the guardians of Earth. That is also why they share the same symbol as the Lemurians. However, it's important to note that some Natives had already lived in the Americas before the Lemurians got here and had their own civilization.

S: *What were the Americas like?*

L: The Americas were home to a very advanced civilization, but that was destroyed.

S: *How was it destroyed?*

L: Through wars and floods.

I was amazed at the knowledge that came through the ancestors and how confirming it was with other sessions I have had. There was no way that Les could have known any of this information. To find out more I had a short session with a client I call Fred.

S: *Could you tell me more about the Americas? Why are they so special?*

F: The Americas were home to many advanced civilizations that were similar to the advanced civilization of the Mayans. These ancient, advanced societies and much of their religion was based on worshipping the sun as they did in Atlantis. The Mayans were heavily influenced by Atlantis and Lemuria. Most of the Mayans ascended, some went to the rainforest, but most left through the stone gateways and ascended into higher realms where they continue to work with humanity or other life on other planets.

S: *If the Americas had an advanced civilization like the Mayans, what happened to the structures in the Americas?*

F: There were many cataclysms and resets and the advanced civilizations built with ancient technology in the Americas were all destroyed. Some of the founding fathers were descendants of the survivors from Atlantis. Some have misused the sacred teachings and have committed crimes against humanity. However, the main problem came from the Atlanteans that went north during that time.

S: *What happened to the people who went north?*

F: Many became obsessed with greed and power.

S: *Well, the question that has been burning in my mind is why did the White Men do such atrocities to the Native Americans? What happened to the White Men?*

F: The White Men were some of the earliest victims of this negative energy that crashed onto this Earth, the Fear virus. Many White Men were the first human hybrid slaves in Atlantis. For many, the White Man's culture was taken from them so long ago that they don't even remember what their culture was or that they even had a culture.

S: *What do you mean? What was their culture before it was taken from them?*

F: Their culture was Paganism; they were witches. They used to dance among fairies and understand the power of the sun. They used to have so many magical beliefs. They used to remember dragons, fairies, they had symbolic dances, and that was their original culture. They lived alongside and in harmony with the Earth just like everyone else's original culture. Some of these practices still exist in Europe today, but for most this was all taken away, and the White Men eventually forgot who they were.

S: *So, all of this is from that fear, that negative influence that arrived on our planet?*

F: Yes. It was opportunistic and found its way into their minds as they started practicing advanced dark ceremonies and were not aware that that was what they were doing. This is why we only give information when humans are ready for it.

S: *So how is that negative influence now?*

F: The negative influence is losing its hold. There are billions of extraterrestrial souls on Earth now, many would call them Star Seeds and they are from all over the universe in order to help the evolution of consciousness. Once these Star Seeds are all brought to awareness about who they are they become even more powerful. **For centuries the negative energy has tried to wipe out the stories, but no matter how hard they tried, they couldn't get rid of the memories. The traditions have survived, and these stories have been waiting, waiting for this time in history to return.**

S: *Why has all of this happened in the way that it did?*

F: The intention was **to create an amazing experiment; to see, not only how humans would separate, but how they would eventually come back together with this information.** This has all been a test, a game, and for us all to unite again, but to unite better and to unite where there is appreciation of the union as well.

*In order to increase the validity of the information I receive I use multiple subjects who have never met one another. **Below is a session with a client named Andy who while deep under hypnosis had a group of beings come through***

claiming to be the descendants of the survivors from Lemuria.

S: *Who am I talking with?*

A: We are a collective. We are the descendants of the survivors of what you would call Lemuria currently living in and out of Mt. Shasta.

S: *Tell me more about that.*

A: After our beloved civilization was destroyed many of us went to the Americas.

S: *Why did you go to the Americas?*

A: We were drawn because of the energy there; we could feel the pull. There are deep crystal chasms within the mountain complex of Mt. Shasta that are very specific and unique to the Earth, and we became aware of them. We could feel the pull towards them. We were aware that they could sustain the life and consciousness that we were searching for. And so, after our beloved home of Lemuria was destroyed, many of us relocated here in Mt. Shasta, California.

S: *What kind of consciousness were you looking for and what did you find?*

A: We were looking for the consciousness and energy within Mt. Shasta. This energy can sustain life without food.

S: *How does the energy sustain life without food?*

A: There are powerful crystals within that mountain that are celestial converters. These crystals have a specific configuration that allows Earth energy to be manifested and magnified in combination with the movement of the planet through the Milky Way galaxy. This energy transitions into life force energy emanating from the crystals. However, this is unique to Mt. Shasta.

S: *Why does Mt. Shasta have these special crystals?*

A: They were placed there by an early group of extra-terrestrials who came before life was seeded on Earth.

S: *Why did they place them there?*

A: They understood the trajectories of the human experience and knew that Lemuria would eventually be destroyed and that many of the Lemurians would go to Mt. Shasta. **This is part of the path and the unfolding of the consciousness of life on Earth. It is part of the cycle and original plan.**

S: *So, this has always been a plan?*

A: Yes.

S: *What is the plan now? What is supposed to happen?*

A: The transition of consciousness. This has been planned since the time of Lemuria and before.

S: *Why was this planned?*

A: Earth is unique in its framework because there are opportunities that come with Earth and with life on Earth and there are various cycles that were planned as part of the unfoldment of this consciousness. Earth has gone through waves, peaks, and valleys, which is just part of that process. **It was always set for Earth to go through this transitionary period you are in now and move into higher spheres of consciousness.**

S: *What can a person do now that this is happening? Is there anything they need to do?*

A: It would greatly benefit all to position their consciousness in the right place, to make sure that they are on the path and timeline that they wish to follow. Not everyone makes the shift into a higher level of consciousness. But if a human desires to shift they can make themselves as light as possible through their thoughts, mind, body, actions, ways of living, purity of consciousness and intention. **Those who move towards inner evolution are already on that journey. Those who seek outside themselves do so at their own peril.**

S: How does your collective feel about what is going on with humanity right now?

A: We feel compassion for the chaos of your time as we retain the memories of the chaos during the destruction of our beloved Lemuria. We have not only retained our memories, but we've also retained our access to the past and we've kept these memories sacred within us. The current experience on Earth is one of complete forgetfulness. And so, within that forgetfulness there is fear that needs inner evolution to navigate it successfully. This we have come to learn since we have already completed our shift.

S: What advice would you give people that would help them with this shift?

A: There are great benefits in developing one's own inner world and moving into contact with one's soul and the light of who they are. It would help greatly to become aware of this light and become intimately involved with the deeper aspects of who you are. Once you become aware of this light within, you realize the truth of everything, and only then can you see through the distortions that are presented within you and around you, in all directions. Once you go within yourself you see that you are eternal, that you are the expression of love made manifest. You are not the personality or the ego, you are light made into life.

S: Do you consider yourself to be human in the mountain?

A: Not in the same way you would consider a human to be. We have evolved past what we consider to be human over the generations. Much of that has to do with the crystals in Mt. Shasta and we've been soaking in that energy for thousands of years. Because of this we can shift in and out of physical reality when needed.

S: When you're not in physical reality where do you go?

A: We have cities of light that appear physical to us, but they would not appear physical to someone who is not at our vibrational frequency.

S: There are many people who remember living in the time of Lemuria.

A: Yes, there are many who remember who are back again to release the fear and trauma that came from that event of losing their beloved home and the uncertainty of that experience and what that was. It was so sudden that it left a psychic wound on the soul. Many souls are back in the physical to do this.

S: *What do they need to do to release this?*

A: This is a time of letting go and moving on, of moving inwards as opposed to outwards. The outward expression of life is just that, just an outward expression. The pains, trials and tribulations that come with the outward expression of life need not be held onto. They should be released, just like the pains of the past need to be released and let go.

S: *Is there a way to do this?*

A: We would say that the most powerful way is done through personal forgiveness. Forgive yourselves.

S: *What could you tell me about the Native Americans and indigenous tribes?*

A: The indigenous tribes all over this Earth planet carry the sacred wisdom that we carry as well, and we still maintain that wisdom.

S: *Does this sacred wisdom originate from Lemuria?*

A: This sacred information is older than Lemuria. It has been passed through Lemuria, passed through the Pleiades before that, and passed through other civilizations and experiences older than those.

S: *What is some of this wisdom that is carried?*

A: The ability to become free within oneself.

S: *How do you do that?*

A: By understanding that on this realm there is duality. Bad things happen as part of being in a physical body in an evolving society and civilization, growing pains if you will. It's important to not let the growing pains injure you along your path of growth and development into love and personal inner evolution. There's an old adage of being like a child, of being light as a feather, of being aware of innocence and willing to tap into your own inner innocence which transcends time. People have forgotten what it is like to be free within themselves.

S: *Can you tell me more about how to become free within yourself?*

A: **You become free when you permeate yourself with a sense of wonder, a sense of connectedness, curiosity, this is key**. It's been forgotten, assaulted, and attacked across the entirety of the human race in order to force people to forget who they are.

S: *What could help the indigenous cultures, the sacred wisdom keepers?*

A: It would benefit all to release their own personal story of tragedy, that is everyone's path forward. Understand that the matriarchal society within the Lemurian civilization came head-to-head with the patriarchal dominance resulting in the loss of the matriarch. Because of this it created imbalance almost like a pendulum swinging from extreme to extreme. Humans are still coming back through that counter swing, back towards a place of balance. In everything there is intention and this coming back into balance allows for a shift.

S: *What will the shift be like for those that experience it?*

A: It's an individual process. Some will experience it more suddenly than others. Others will gradually move into it as old aspects of their life fade away, and then there are those who will awaken to the full potential of themselves and just see through everything. It's not uniform. It unfolds in the way that an individual perceives and processes this. There's a lot of individuality as part of that.

S: *What will it be like after the shift?*

A: Manifesting things will be significantly easier. The transition time from thought to action into physical manifestation will be significantly sped up.

S: *Is there anything that Andy will notice?*

A: Body changes. He's already experiencing them. Some foods will no longer be in resonance with him or in resonance with his desire to deepen his inner resolve within himself and his connection to his physicality.

S: *Does the shift affect you, the Lemurian collective?*

A: We're isolated from it. We've already made this shift. And so, when we come back through, we are lowering ourselves back into the physical form of life. And when we leave, we move back into those higher states.

S: *Why do you come back into Mt. Shasta? Why not just stay in your city of light?*

A: It's our agreement that we would hold this space energetically, as a pathway for others to follow. We are the lineage of consciousness from the old to the new. So, within our civilization, and our agreement with the Earth, and because we have the original memories of Lemuria and have maintained and honored them, we serve as the transition point from the old into the new. Part of Earth's evolution is the transition from physical to higher physical. To help others along that path and that journey, we as a group have agreed to come and go between those two states of awareness. And because we've been through it, we hold it internally within us and this helps others to do the same. This is much like what you would call the 100th monkey effect. This is how we can help humanity through our experiences. Many survivors from Lemuria came here to Mt. Shasta but there were some who went to other parts of America, as well as Australia, according to where they were drawn or placed. There were different soul groups who took different evolutionary paths.

S: *What about the soul groups from Atlantis?*

A: Many went to the Americas or Egypt, and some spread out throughout the world. Many still have harsh lessons for themselves that they're still working out to resolve.

S: *What lessons are they still working out?*

A: Many people who once had a lifetime in Atlantis still to this day work for a less than positive situation on the planet.

S: Why are they doing this still?

A: At a soul level they are still seeking resolution. However, in our opinion they could find connection with their higher consciousness and understand that they are not just physical beings. This is not in fact a physical world but just a projection. They act as if they are the rulers of physicality, which is foolish. For they are no more the rulers of physical reality than an ant or a fish is. The abusive masculine energy has reincarnated through them to be faced, integrated, and brought back into balance, and transformed within them. That was the goal and why they have returned. It would help them to acknowledge the divine within them and around them. Many of them have shut themselves off from the higher faculties of spirit, which allows them to hurt and injure others without compassion, without feeling for what they're doing or concern for others or the planet. Those who intentionally hurt others have a rude awakening coming.

S: Why do they have a rude awakening?

A: They may end up on the negative polarity of the shift. This shift will show them the demonstration of how their choices and decisions unfold.

S: If you look at the Mandela effect, it seems as if you can focus and experience a different reality according to your focus. Is this correct?

A: Yes. The Mandela effect is multifaceted. There are aspects of it that are a result of the bleeding over of simultaneous time, parallel realities and intentional time travel that is changing things in the past at a subtle or micro level. But yes, the Mandela effect is proof that you can change your own timeline.

S: So, a person could literally create their own path then?

A: Yes, that is very correct. **Humans are creating their own experiences in every moment and while outside influence can affect this at times, ultimately the human is the one who is in charge of their experience.**

S: Can the Grey extra-terrestrials really change timelines?

A: Not just the Greys, but many extra-terrestrials can.

S: What if they change your timeline?

A: This happens regularly. Most humans are not aware and simply follow the new timeline that has changed and shifted for them. But there is always a choice. They can go down the new path or carry on with the old. It's harder to force realities on them if they are self-aware. The human involved is not consciously aware but has agreed on a subconscious level.

S: What would the point of changing timelines be?

A: Different agendas by different groups.

S: Tell me more.

A: There are many different groups with many different agendas. Some groups would not like humanity to shift and expand their consciousness and other groups do. There are many different groups, however, and the Grey extra-terrestrial has multiple forms, much like humans, and there are different interpretations of that form throughout the multiverse. They are not uniform per se, you have different races and civilizations. Some of which are in higher states of awareness, higher states of evolution, and others are not. So, it's not necessarily a uniform situation when it comes to any group.

S: Are there any beings that would be most considered the future versions of humanity?

A: There are plenty of extra-terrestrial races considered to be humanity's future but we, the ascended group in Mt. Shasta consider ourselves to be one of the future potentials of the human evolution as we have bridged the gap from the past to the present, into the future.

S: Do you have any other advice for humans?

A: Be gentler on the pains of what it means to be a human. Personal judgement is a huge problem within humanity. Letting go of that personal judgement and truly learning what it means to love oneself will change everything. It's the pains that are held onto which injure and reinjure human beings. There's a need to let go of what that is, to re-embrace that innocence and childlike wonder. However, the opposite has been ingrained by society for eons for control.

S: *What can a human do then?*

A: Reconnecting with self-love. It starts there.

S: *Could you tell me more about the advanced civilizations in the Americas? What were they like?*

A: There are groups of civilizations that share this space with us although you would have to be attuned to that same frequency to see them. So, there are still some advanced civilizations in the Americas which you could not see but are still there. Some of these advanced civilizations in the Americas have transitioned, much like we have or similar to how the Mayans did. Many of those transitions took place in smaller groups like ours, however what is being intended now is for a large group shift. That is the difference between now and what has come before in the past.

S: *So, this will be a large shift and those who shifted before were small groups. What about the advanced structures that were in the Americas then, where are they?*

A: Many of the advanced structures in the Americas were buried or destroyed. When the Americas were set up and established, the intention was to leave the old world, old patterns, old school of thought behind and bring its own intention of spiritual freedom. That was the original intention for the Americas. And it was built into the fabric of America's original creation, as a modern country. However, the Native people within their civilizations who maintained their connection in relationship to the Earth have always had a place in the Americas.

S: *Whose idea was it for the America's to be the birthplace of spiritual freedom?*

A: This was designed by Source. The human collective chose this, and the energetic grid system allowed for this. Much of the Americas were founded by those who fled other places, whether that be the Lemurian civilization, or the European civilizations who fled seeking personal freedoms or escape from the old world, or the Atlanteans who were able to flee before the destructions.

S: *What happened when the White Men took over and destroyed so much?*

A: This was all part of the cycle and represented through symbols. **Man moved further away from the land and further away from oneness and moved towards civilized progress and technological development. Man will once again return back to the land and back to oneness. It's just a continuous up and down movement of moving away from oneness and then back to it.**

S: *How were the humans able to go from these places that they fled from to the Americas?*

A: Many were taken on ships or crafts, but they do not have any conscious memories of this while they were moved. Some of those groups that were moved had specific beliefs or understandings or latent energetics that were important for the unfolding of the new civilizations or new societies they were moved to.

S: *Is there anything else that you would like to share?*

A: We would just like to acknowledge that this is a very exciting time for the human race. This has been a long time coming. Many long-standing patterns are being undone and transformed.

S: *What do you mean?*

A: The previous waves of Star Seeds have come here in the physical flesh to steer the ship in a different direction, and it is working. There are changes happening, changes in thinking, and the old ways of thought are dissolving. This is the dissolution of the old and the uncovering of that which was hidden. These are very exciting times for the Earth right now.

S: *Why does everything have to be done in the physical? I mean I know that's part of this experience, but why is it that way?*

A: This is part of the agreement for this Earth planet. When Earth was made there were certain rules that were created around it and a path or direction that the Earth would take. So, within that framework there were rules that were established, such as the experience of gravity, polarity, being born and dying. These were some of the opportunities that came with the Earth and this physical experiment. The rules of the Earth were designed and developed all around this evolutionary experiment that was to take place here.

S: *And the Native Americans are the sacred knowledge keepers. Is there anything else that is important about that?*

A: Yes. They understood what the consciousness of the Earth represented. **The consciousness of the Earth is simply another expression of the consciousness of God, the consciousness of love, the consciousness of creation, and how that plays itself out.** This is all about the vast and rich history of the human journey here on Earth and where they are headed. Humans need to release their judgement of the negative polarity and understand that it is part of the learning dichotomy of Earth. **The experiment on Earth is designed that way and within that expression is free will and a choice whether we perceive it to be positive or negative. From our perspective it is all the same, it's all part of the same circle of life.** However, the negative polarity lives in unconsciousness, but you do not have consciousness without unconsciousness. They feed into each other. It will benefit all humans to stop, let go, and stop running away from the pains of the world and see the world as it is. **It's hard to see so much pain inflicted on others and it's hard not to judge the source of this pain. But it has a purpose, and that purpose leads inwards towards personal growth and accountability and it may not always be immediate, but the growth never leaves. It always comes back, it always transforms, it always delivers itself upwards. That's the cycle of life, the circle, and so it's simply part of the unfolding journey. It's a tool within the threshold of inward and outward expansion and expression. It's the emotions that human beings experience which causes the perception of it being good or bad, wrong, or right, positive, or negative. In reality, they simply transition** into each other, and this is the circle, the cycle, and the sacred knowledge.

CHAPTER 7:
THE NEGATIVE POLARTIY

If the White Men were early victims of this negative polarity, then what about humanity at this moment? I wanted to find out more, so I had Mary come in for a session. Here is her session.

M: If you look through the Orion's and the Pleiades star systems, there are beings there that we could call the ancestors of the human race. There was a planet that was seeded by these beings that no longer supports life. We're just going to call these people the Pleiadeans. The planet, we will call Terra.

S: *Are these the real names or why do you want to call them this?*

M: Just so that it could be recognizable as there are many different names for these places.

S: *Ok, can you tell me more about this planet that you want to call Terra?*

M: This was very much like Earth as there were streams, water, sun, and it shared the same central sun as Earth. There was what you would call magic there. The beings were very tall and had elongated faces. These are the types of beings that we're talking about that are one of the ancestors of the humans. We will call these people the Pleiadeans, just to give them a name. This planet within the Pleiades was not completely taken over at first but there was some discord in the galaxy. There was a nefarious group and some of them came from the Orion star system. Not all of the Orions were of integrity. Some of the Orions had intentions of greed and they had already taken over other planets before. The Orions didn't want to take over the Pleiades because their planet within the Orion star system was destroyed or that they needed to take a planet because they had nowhere to live, but in fact they wanted to own this area of the galaxy because they could control the beings that would travel through that part of the galaxy. Earth was not a planet that was inhabited by humans at that time. Earth was going through its own transition. It was also carrying that which you would know as early dinosaurs at this time. Earth had reptile beings that were connected to the draconian and the reptilian family. During this time the beings from Terra had to leave their planet within the Pleiades and find somewhere else to live. Some refugees went to what you call Mars, but the Mars that you see now was not like the Mars that was present at that time. Mars had oxygen and water, and many of the refugees tried to seed themselves on Mars. But when that was destroyed, they then moved over to planet Earth. And that is where they began to create new families, create new colonies. At this time there were connections to the cosmos through vibrational crystals, alignment with the stars, and through metals like gold and silver. They had many different ways of communicating with the Star beings, as there were many others in the Pleiades who would keep in contact with these people.

S: *Did these beings originally come from the Pleiades?*

M: Yes. The Orion group wanted power and to take over that area. This is very much the story of darkness and light. So, we could also say that this is very much the story of the angels and the dark side, one side wanting to take over the other. Earth was also part of this galaxy, and so therefore Earth was of interest to these darker beings as well. It was not a welcoming idea that these Pleiadeans would reseed themselves on Earth because there they would be able to spread light and spreading light would mean that they would be able to gain control and gain power. And at that time, the negative polarity was also attempting to seed their own beings, which we would recognize as the reptilians.

S: *Oh, so the reptilians were the negative polarity's seeded beings? Then what happened?*

M: There were other beings that had come to the Earth. Some were not Pleiadean, some people would call them Anunnaki, although this can also be a broad term for many early seeders of the Earth planet. But the ones we're talking about were of a darker polarity and were coming for the purpose of greed and with intentions of control. This is when humans started to see heaven on Earth starting to change. This is where we start to see the human being shifting away from their awareness, starting to have separation. This would also be the time of Atlantis, a time when the water started to take over the Earth, when many beings had to leave for cover, and leave the areas where they had seeded themselves. This is when there was great change on the Earth and a disconnection from the divine self, from the Prime Creator.

S: *Why?*

M: It was because of the introduction of the energy of greed and negative energy, not by punishment, not by force, but by the choice to experience. And the prime energy, or as some would call God, allowed this experience to take place and over time there was a disconnection for the human from the higher realms.

S: *So, when humans were first seeded on this planet, they had a higher connection then?*

M: Yes, and many lived in the place you call Lemuria.

S: *Okay. Were humans designed to be easily controlled?*

M: No. Humans are equipped with polarity as is true of everything on Earth. Humans are equipped with the mind and over many generations, the mind begins to develop itself and learns from generations previous and becomes repetitive. And so, the human being becomes easier to convince. And over generations humans become less connected to the divine self.

S: *Ok. So, what happened to the Lemurians?*

M: Their continent was destroyed, however there were survivors who trickled into the native cultures around the world.

S: *So, all that wisdom is stored within the native tribes. Is that correct?*

M: That is correct and what is happening now is that this information is resurfacing. There are many open lines of communication, downloads, and activation of DNA. Due to the planetary shifting, the recalibration of the polarity, recalibration of the masculine and feminine energy, and the cellular memory that is carried through the individuals that are human and physically present on Earth right now, the humans here are embodying this energy on Earth to bring forward this wisdom into action.

S: *And do you get a sense as to what wisdom is important for people to understand?*

M: Going back to nature, going back to the self, drawing back from what is given to you on the outside, because what is on the outside is an illusion. **The wisdom of your ancestors winding through many generations and reaching back up into the stars is a memory of a compassionate, yet strong warrior, one that is able to think for thy self, and one that is able to honor the Earth.**

S: *Why could the Natives see the faery people, or the Little People as they called them, but the White Man couldn't?*

M: This was because the natives kept their culture, beliefs, and their ceremonies very sacred and private. And through many generations, that belief system would be held together. Everything in reality is seeded from the belief system of the individual. And so, as many human beings go through different cultures, different generations, they become less and less connected to that realm. Some will only see the Little People in books, and some will never see them at all. So, it would all depend on their belief system.

S: *Oh, is that why the Natives could see the extraterrestrials and the White Man had trouble?*

M: That is correct, however, the White Man used to have magical practices and beliefs before it was taken from them for control.

All of this was so confirming as this matched up to the other sessions I've had.

S: *I have been told that the Galactic Federation protects the Earth now. And this is a battle between light and dark over and over and over again. How does it look now?*

M: Because time is not linear, we have already seen timelines where the war has already been won. There are also timelines where we are existing now through the process of winning, through the process of moving forward. What happens in the present time affects the outcome, not necessarily the outcome of whether or not we have won the war, but how long this will take and how it will play out. Now, what we would like to explain is that there have been many galactic wars fought over light versus dark for many billions of years and many of the souls that are playing today are the very same souls that have played long ago. The dark players are trying to take over Earth through technology and modern advancements so that they can create a world where not only do they have control, but they can experience luxury. Part of this negative energy does experience pleasure and seeks it at all costs, not fully understanding that there is another way of taking pleasure of experiencing joy through the light. And so, the Galactic Federation is highly involved in what happens with the Earth, because what happens with the Earth affects the universe around it. It affects the entirety, it affects other planets, it also affects the future of other beings. And so, there is great interest and assistance for the Earth at this time.

S: *Why can't there be more intervention? Why can't these Star People help more than they do?*

M: They do in ways that are not recognized by humans. One could say there are many things that are already being done, that many human beings are not able to see, or able to understand, even the ones that have more conscious awareness. When there's any type of war going on, there are always certain things that the opponent is not to know. There are sometimes steps that are not taken because these steps are being savored for a particular moment in time.

S: *Okay. I would really like to know about the cattle mutilations. I've heard that this is a nefarious group that performs these; could tell me more about this?*

M: There are a couple of different reasons as to why these cattle mutilations occur. Some of it is experimentation. Some of it is also for DNA. There are beings that are part of, we will say, the darker energy, that work alongside humans, and they do not look at the cattle as intelligent beings. We can also see that they use lasers as a way to perform this mutilation. Most humans would not believe that this would happen, but the cattle are lifted off the ground in order to excrete certain parts. There are some cattle that are missing certain parts, there are some that are being cut in certain directions, and much of this has to do with the **study of the cattle connected with the growth of human consciousness.**

S: *What do you mean by that?*

M: Many humans consume meat from cattle. This is not a judgment, as we do not judge or place judgment on anyone that consumes meat. However, what we will say is that meat product is not the highest vibration to consume. There is a study of what is being put into meat by this more nefarious group of beings to create a substance within meat that will help dull the consciousness of the human being.

S: *Are these human beings or extra-terrestrials doing this?*

M: They are humans with help from a darker nefarious energy. Some are not fully aware of who they are connected to. We speak of some scientists, and some doctors that are not aware of the full connection and that they are not fully aware of the agenda. If you were to look at your hand and say that the palm of the hand is this nefarious group, then each finger represents the different components such as the scientists, doctors, and other people who create certain studies in order to feed information. But these separate entities do not know of each other or realize that they are in a sense connected to the hand.

S: *So, the cattle mutilations are done by a nefarious group of humans trying to take different parts of the cattle.*

M: That is correct. Also, you will notice that the DNA extracted is only from the left side of the cow because this would be where the more aggressive masculine side resides. This is where a lot of the energy able to slow down the human frequency would be. The right side is the more feminine side and is constantly expanding its frequency and integrating with the left side.

S: *How do they lift these cattle up so high in the air and why do they go about doing that?*

M: They do this with a tool that looks like a light that is used to suspend the animal. Lifting the animal is important in order to see through the cow and its entirety so that they can see the animal almost like a grid. In this way they can see temperatures, even down to the percentage of the fertilizer that the cow has ingested.

S: *Why are there no footprints around anywhere when these cattle mutilations occur?*

M: The mutilation happens while the cattle are suspended so there is no actual physical connection with the ground.

S: *So, this is to extract certain things from the cattle to then figure out how to put it into the meat humans eat in order to dull the human mind. Correct?*

M: Yes. They call it a harvesting process.

S: *Okay, anything else about that that you notice?*

M: There are other things that they are working on, but this would be one that we're able to share. There are humans who do perform experiments on humans as well. They look to test the results of their experiments and there are some humans that are being followed and studied. Some of these humans are those who have disappeared, and some are humans who are taken for brief periods of time during their slumber or feel that they have time missing in their day. They may not realize that they are being drawn to certain foods, that they are being experimented on in how they exist in the world with their energy after they ingest certain foods. They are studied to see how these foods and other substances are affecting their vibration and their consciousness, and how controllable they are. And what is difficult for many of these human beings who are experiencing this is that there have been generations of them that become paranoid because they are recognizing that something is not right. They're having experiences where they're seeing some of these people show up in their bedrooms at night, or they are having memories of being in some sort of medical facility with people that they do not recognize. Many of them are called crazy, they are called tinfoil hats or people that have a screw loose. And so, it becomes very difficult for them to prove their experiences.

S: *What could help people like that?*

M: Well as the consciousness shifts, and the ascension and awakening process continues to take place, as each human being is beginning to reach their mass light quota, this is going to help create not only the individual realities but begin to continue to expand a collective reality which will start to expose some of the conditions that have been submerged below the radar.

S: *What else will become exposed?*

M: Much of history in its true form is emerging and with that the old language of symbols, which originated from the Star People.

S: *Which symbols?*

M: Symbols such as the Scarab symbol and the Eye of Horus were used by the Atlanteans, and this is not widely known by the general public.

S: *Those symbols came from Atlantis?*

M: They came from the Galactic Federation but were used in Atlantis and then brought to ancient Egypt after some survivors escaped the cataclysm. The Eye of Horus is a symbol meaning that the creator is always watching even during the wars that took place throughout our history. This symbol reminds humanity that there is always a watching eye. Some would call it the divine eye. This symbol is an energetic symbol that was created and has traveled through humanity. Some would consider this a symbol of the third eye as well.

S: *What about the Scarab symbol?*

M: This too, comes from a collective, a galactic source that holds this sacred information. The Scarab symbol has a consciousness that is connected to a sacred feminine energy.

S: *Are there any other symbols that appear important from these ancient cultures?*

M: We see the Four Corners symbol as important.

S: *Tell me about that.*

M: The Four Corners symbol relates to the four elements, fire, water, earth, and air as well as the four directions, north, east, west, and south. This symbol contains sacred information. It is a carrier of this consciousness, and the symbol is a way to travel with information and a way to send information or conjure information and conjure protection.

S: *Do you notice anything else about this sacred symbol of the Four Corners?*

M: We're also able to see that it can change shape. It can change the way that it presents itself.

S: *What do you mean by that?*

M: This sacred symbol of the Four Corners can change shape according to not only the intention, but the element, the temperature, the circumstance, and the need for protection.

S: *When it changes shape, does it look different?*

M: Yes, when this sacred symbol needs to protect the information, it can look like a shield.

All of the information that I received from Mary was very confirming. Below is another session with Les as Aniwaya describes more of his harrowing journey on the Trail of Tears.

CHAPTER 8: THE HORRORS OF THE TRAIL

As Aniwaya delved deeper into the memories of the Trail of Tears, his memories were heartbreaking.

S: *Tell me more about the Trail.*

L: Sometimes the overwhelming feeling of guilt would hit me as I looked at my people walking because I felt like I had failed, not only myself, but the entire nation, all of my people. Sometimes while I walked the Trail, I wished that I could go back in time to figure out a way when I was in England to have someone listen to us, even though I knew that it was impossible. There were just so many deaths, old people, young people, and there were many diseases that we suffered from. The White Men gave us blankets at one point, and these blankets would make us cough and sneeze.

S: *Why?*

L: Now looking at it from a different perspective I can see that there was bacteria on these blankets from the rats that had come over on their ships. Their ships were dirty, and these rats were diseased and would either defecate or just lie on these blankets before these blankets were given to us.

S: *What type of diseases did these blankets cause?*

L: The diseases sucked the life out of my people and often caused a bad cough and congestion. We had remedies for this, but they never let us walk off the Trail to pick anything. So, we couldn't help each other. I had some medicine in my pouch that I carried around my neck, but this had been given to me by my mother and it was the last thing that I had of hers. I had carried it all my life, but at one point I had to give it to the woman I loved. I gave her the last of my medicine and the last physical trace of my mother that I carried.

S: *Tell me more.*

L: I had carried that medicine for so many years that I knew that it would be powerful because of the meaning behind it. The woman I loved became very weak. I prayed and asked that I wouldn't lose her; I couldn't lose her. I felt as if I would just give up if she didn't make it. My mother came to me and told me to give her the medicine that I was carrying, that it was the only way. It was a hard decision. I knew my mother would still be around me in spirit, but I didn't want to lose the last thing I had from her. I could still feel my mother's energy in that pouch that I carried. And so, I decided that it was the only way, and I crushed it with two stones, and I ground it up and boiled it in a tea.

S: *Did it help her?*

L: It did, but slowly. She was very ill and even though the medicine was working she was still so weak that I had to carry her for many miles until she recovered.

As a regressionist I've heard many tragic things over the years, but nothing has ever before brought tears to my eyes. Below is more of Aniwaya's detailed accounts of walking the Trail of Tears.

L: There were so many deaths, but the first death was early on in our walking. She was a wise and valuable elder in our tribe, but she was too frail to walk. She knew that it would be a long road and not wanting to burden us she sat down on the Trail. The White Men were so mean and said that if anyone refused to walk then they would be shot and that was exactly what they did. They took a pistol to her head and shot her in front of us all.

S: Did your whole tribe see her get shot?

L: Yes, to our shock and horror and in front of us all, including our children, she was shot in the head. It was very graphic and close enough that I noticed that I had some of her brains on me. It wasn't a lot, but enough to upset my stomach any time I looked at it. I remember some of it got on my chest and I just couldn't stop looking at it in horror! It had a terrible smell too and I couldn't believe that it was hers. I couldn't believe these people would do this! These people didn't realize that they are just like us. I couldn't believe that these people could do the horrible things that they did.

S: What else did they do?

L: These people would do horrific things to us. The soldiers would constantly rape the women when we would set up camp and I couldn't do anything to stop it. There were many, many children who died on the Trail. There were children that were even born on the Trail. It was very difficult because if a mother started going into labor while we were walking, they wouldn't stop and so we would have to band together. All of us would band together, like maybe ten or fifteen of us, and lift her up and carry her, so that way she could give birth. We would all try to encourage her and support her, but it was very difficult and a lot of the times the baby wouldn't make it because of the stress. And sometimes the mother wouldn't make it because of the same thing. And the soldiers didn't want us to have babies anyway. They did such horrible, horrible things to us. Sometimes they would rip a crying baby away from its mother and the mother would just scream as they threw the baby into the river. They were always trying to show us how little they cared. They wanted to break us. And some of us did.

S: What was this like for your tribe?

L: Some of us started to become numb and I felt numb.

S: Tell me more.

L: There were children that were shot just for target practice or some who got sick and died because they were so little and didn't have enough fat on their bodies to continue. Food was so scarce that our bodies relied on the stored muscle that we had and some of the small children just could not make it. We would often take turns carrying the smaller ones. It was not a burden to carry the children at all; it was a blessing really. To have that soul so close to us while we were walking gave us something to walk for. But we did see children die, many children. Out of our tribe most of the people who died were children and our elderly, but there were many, many people who passed of all different ages. However, **as we walked and grew wearier our energies and vibration got lower and lower and that is when the Skin Walkers started showing up on the Trail.**

S: *What do you mean?*

L: The Skin Walkers were attracted to the low vibration, but it was worse for the White Man than it was for us.

S: *Tell me more. What are Skin Walkers?*

L: The Skin Walker is a nefarious type of energy. Some would know it as a shapeshifter. It tends to shift inter-dimensionally, and shift from a humanoid to an animal humanoid. It is very old, and very primitive. We can compare it to being connected to many ancient, old energies that are currently working on the Earth and working in many different ways, shapes, and forms to help the darker forces feed off of fear. They are more like worker bees in that they create fear, and that fear carries a frequency that they're able to feed off of and then bring forth to the queen bee.

S: *Were they human at one point, or were they just an energy form?*

L: They are a mixture of both. They are from an energetic source, but they are of a humanoid origin. And so, they do have a human type of energy with them. There are some that have had a human life at one point in time that has been taken in by this nefarious energy. Human beings can excrete an energetic frequency from themselves due to something that they may have experienced through what would be called a dark life. And when that human being passes, they can choose to stay in that frequency, and they can then start to begin to develop into something that is married with the energy of what we would call the Skin Walker.

S: *And then there are also the ancient groups that are benevolent, correct?*

L: Correct, but the Skin Walkers started to torment the White Men on the Trail.

S: *Why?*

L: It wasn't because we were being favored over the White Man, but because we carried an energy of respecting tradition. And so, because there is a humanoid presence in the Skin Walker, and many of us had generations of respecting the Earth and the space that we were on, the Skin Walker wanted to create fear for the group that smelled to them like the enemy. We smelled to them as something similar to themselves, so the White Men were more tempting.

S: *What would they do when they started showing up?*

L: They would create more fear through their strange noises within the forest. There were some men that went into the forest looking for the strange noises who never returned. It felt at times like the whole world mourned for us, even the people we passed by would sometimes cry as they saw us.

S: *Tell me more.*

L: They could see this horror, and it was said that where we shed our tears, the Cherokee rose would bloom and that's why they named it the Cherokee rose, even though it doesn't really look like a rose.

S: *Tell me more about this rose?*

L: The Cherokee rose was very symbolic, as is all of nature, and this rose symbolized proof of the divine spirit within us all. There are seven leaves on the Cherokee rose symbolizing the seven clans of the Cherokee. The center of the blossom represented a pile of gold to remind us of the White Man's greed for the gold found on our homeland. This was one of the main reasons that they wanted to take our lands, but this symbolic flower is sturdy and strong with stickers on all the stems. Symbolically it will defy anything that tries to destroy it. These flowers still bloom along the Trail to this day.

As I was transcribing this session a very strange phenomenon happened to me. I noticed that while working on this section my left eye was very watery. It didn't make any sense. My eyes were not irritated at all and so I looked in the mirror to see what was causing my left eye to be so watery. When I looked at my reflection, I saw that there were tears coming out of my eye and were rolling all the way down my face! It isn't uncommon to have all kinds of strange anomalies happen to me while working on these books, but this one felt very symbolic.

S: *What kinds of things did you and your tribe talk about as you walked? It must have been just devastating.*

L: At first, we would talk a lot about where we thought we were going, but as time went on, we stopped talking. Talking took up a lot of energy and we didn't want to waste any energy that we could save. Even just talking with our mouths became very taxing; however, we realized that we were so connected that we could communicate with our minds, and we started to sing our songs together silently. We started to do this on a daily basis, and this gave us strength. Sometimes we would hum, but if we hummed too loud, we would be beaten. And so, we would sing mostly in our heads, and we would continue walking.

S: *Was Black Fox with you on the Trail?*

L: He didn't start out with us. He was so light on his feet that he left the group silently one night before we left but ended up coming back to continue walking with us much later on. I knew that if I wanted to, I could escape too because I was very light on my feet as well and could walk without sound. When I was younger the members of my tribe used to say that I could blend in with the background and almost make myself invisible, but it was just that I could move so quietly. It was an art form that I perfected in order to become an efficient hunter. But I couldn't leave my people and if they were going to walk then I was too. I wasn't going to leave them and especially not the woman that I was in love with. I couldn't live with myself if I did that. Black Fox did return, however. He showed up one night out of the blue many miles and months from where we started, claiming that he realized what I meant when I said that I couldn't leave our people, and so we walked the rest of the way together.

S: *Did Black Fox ever have a family or wife?*

L: Yes, he found a union with the daughter of a chief. Black Fox's father-in-law was not only a chief, but also a very good man. He was faced with the decision to walk or not and this was such a difficult decision for any chief to make. Before walking and after I arrived back from England, the chief and I spoke about our options. If we did not walk, they would destroy our village and kill everyone. I remember what a difficult conversation this was. One night before they came to force us out of our beloved land, we performed a ceremony asking to speak with the **Seven Sisters, the Star People who were our ancestors.** And when we did, they said that it was our choice. We argued with them because we wanted a real answer. But **they said that the choice would have to be ours, and so reluctantly, we chose the way of preservation. It was agreed that if we did this, if we walked, our sacred knowledge would not be lost although we would have to be the keepers of this knowledge until the time was right.**

S: *So, your choices were to not walk and fight or walk and preserve your tribe and the knowledge?*

L: Right, to not walk and risk the lives of our children, wives, mothers, and our fathers and all of the important knowledge we carried with us through word of mouth, or to walk and hope that we made it to where we were being taken. We chose to walk because our tribes had been fighting the White Man for so long and we had lost so many people, so many friends, and we didn't want to lose anyone else. **We knew however, that it really wasn't the White people we were fighting but the negative energy that had them in their control.** Some of the tribe did go underground with the

Nunnehi (the little fairy people), but for us, we knew that we needed to be the ones to carry this information and be the knowledge keepers for when it was needed, which is now.

S: So, the Star People said that you wouldn't lose the information if you walked?

L: Yes, because we knew we were the guardians of this sacred knowledge that needed to be continued. We also knew that the sacred knowledge that we carried was carried from mother to daughter and so we did everything we could to continue that. According to our legends the knowledge was carried through the DNA, the XX chromosome. This knowledge originally came from the Star People. That is where you will find alterations in our DNA.

S: What alterations?

L: Our forefathers had a difference in their DNA that allowed them to connect back to the other side, the Star People, and that DNA and abilities trickled down to us. That was one of the reasons why we had the connection we did to the Earth and our ancestors.

S: Was there anything else as far as knowledge goes that was important for you to continue?

L: We knew that some of this knowledge was hidden in our stories, and it was one of the reasons why the stories were so important. They were coded so that the right information would not get into the wrong hands.

S: What kind of information was this?

L: Surprisingly as I look at this from a different perspective, some of it was how special stones and crystals were, and that spirits could embody a rock or crystal and could be used for healing and energy. Our ancestors would use these stones to build structures that could magnify the electrical current around us. We were aware that when we would dance in spirit it would create an energy around the stone structure creating a portal where people would see visions. Often you could see people transform into their spirit animal while dancing around these stones. My spirit animal was a wolf, and some people would even say that they would see me as a wolf while I danced. I think that's because instead of looking at me with their eyes they were looking at me through their spiritual eye.

S: *What other knowledge was important?*

L: Important knowledge about the medicinal and psychedelic properties of plants was important. You can find a cure for any illness and an answer for any question within nature and we were aware of this. We also used plants in ways that would connect us deeper with spirit in ceremonial practices. We used them by smoking them and by boiling different roots, mushrooms and leaves into a tea that would give you a psychedelic effect. When in this type of ceremony, we would meditate and focus, creating a path within our minds, like a bridge between here and there. And through this bridge we could walk into the spirit world.

S: *What sort of things would you see when you did these ceremonies?*

L: We would see many things; sometimes we saw our loved ones who had passed, especially when we did this for the first time. We would see our loved ones as gatekeepers and as personifications of love. So that way we would know and trust that this was real, and this was a safe place to be. However, this place could manifest your thoughts instantly. And so, you would have to keep yourself calm, because if you started feeling anxious you would start attracting beings who fed off of that anxious energy and fear. Only certain people could smoke this or drink this tea because it was required that you first had control of your mind in order to handle it. Otherwise, it could have detrimental effects. There were stories of people who had done it too soon. And usually, we would wait until the Earth gave us a sign as a token and as proof that we were ready.

S: *So many of you were aware that there were beings that were attracted to fear?*

L: Oh yes. We knew that this negative energy that had control of many of the White Men could come in many forms and they could come to people when the people invited these lower vibrational feelings of fear. There were many rituals to dispel fear or hurt or lower vibration. There were still beings that fed off of these lower vibrational feelings, but we recognized that we created some of these beings ourselves. And some of the things that were plaquing us were from our own creation.

S: *Did you talk about or have a specific way to raise your vibration? Or a practice to dispel the fear?*

L: It was easy for us to achieve a high vibration, especially through our dances and our drums. We could easily feel ourselves lifting higher. We also knew that staying in gratitude is one of the highest vibrational feelings that you can have next to love. As we showed our love to the Earth the Earth would give it back and we would raise our vibration that way.

S: *Was there a method to your dancing? Did you move in any particular direction?*

L: We would. It depended on what we were doing. If we were doing a circle dance, we would dance counterclockwise, but the movement of the dance depended on what the dance was for.

S: *Why the circle?*

L: The circle is sacred. Spheres and circles mimic cycles and time. Real magic happens though if there are two concentric circles moving in opposite directions in prayer. One representing the circle of time and one representing the Earth's cycles.

S: *Tell me more.*

L: If we were trying to praise the beings on the other side or thanking them, we would go back and forth with our dancing. We did this to get their attention, almost like a wave. But if we were trying to create a portal, we would go in one direction continuously for a certain number of times, then we would change the direction. This was done to create balance as with every action there is a reaction. And this could, with the use of certain stones, create a portal. And through the electricity of the dance our brain waves would move into the theta states while we would dance and drum.

In this way there was electricity created and we became conductors and would get the attention of our family in the stars.

S: *What would happen once you created that portal? Would these beings all of a sudden start communicating with you? Or no?*

L: Yes. They would communicate. Sometimes we would see them. I could see them.

S: *What did they look like?*

L: It's hard to explain because they looked like they had so many colors, within an outline of a human, but the main color was a blueish color. They were still humanoid looking, but they did that so that they could try to appear to us in a way that we could understand. Many of us could see them, but you couldn't see their skin. You would see through them because they possessed so much energy that that was the only way that they could manifest themselves. I saw them as colorful outlines in the sky with the stars shining through them. It looked like they were within a blanket of stars.

S: *What colors did you see in them?*

L: They had many colors even though they were see-through, but like I said before, they were mostly blue, but almost like a shadow.

S: *Did they communicate with you?*

L: They would, but through our minds. They would often appear in the center of the circle within the smoke of the fire. They would talk to all of us simultaneously through our minds, all saying the same words. Not everyone could see them, only people who were willing to see them. So it wasn't that others weren't worthy, it was just that they weren't ready. It could be frightening to see these Star People and so that was why the person had to be prepared. This started a big misconception with many different races and cultures that the priest or spiritual leader was better than others because they could communicate with other beings. But it wasn't true that they were better. It was really just that they were ready and could stand the electricity that was being used in their body for the communication with these Star Beings. It was very taxing on the body afterwards and there were other side effects from tuning into that electricity.

S: *Could you tell me more about your ceremonies? Did you always use psychedelics?*

L: Psychedelics were used, but not always. When they were used, they were used as one of the many tools that the creator has given us for our greater understanding. When they were used it was to open the mind rather than close it. One would have to set the intention when using the psychedelics or it could go terribly wrong.

S: *Tell me more about these ceremonies.*

L: Tobacco was used as an offering to give back to the Earth. Sage or clearing plants were used to cleanse the space before the ceremony. This was important to us because we believed that you have to clear the energy before using the space when bringing in higher beings so that only the beings with the highest intention could come into the space. It was also important for our people to sit around the circle representing the four directions, but people could change their forms when they did these dances and ceremonies and that is why it was so important to have a shaman or someone as a guide while we performed these ceremonies. The guide was someone who could walk in the spirit world. If you don't have a shaman, you could get lost and be consumed with the fear that consumed the White Man.

S: *Tell me more.*

L: That is why it's important for us to have someone who has walked through the spirit world, almost like someone holding a candle in the darkness. A shaman learns to carry a torch wherever they go, but it's a spiritual torch that lives inside of us. We all know the way; the only difference is that the shaman has devoted every moment of their lives to building that path. The shaman is a bridge between worlds.

S: *What do you mean that they walk between worlds?*

L: It is similar to what the Little People and Sasquatch do. A shaman learns how these things are done and can move in and out of dimensions. There are thousands of worlds and dimensions that overlap this one. There are also portals to other parts of this universe that a shaman learns to navigate.

S: *How do they learn this?*

L: They devote their lives to learning this, but all one has to do to understand this information is to listen deeply to themselves as that is where you will always find the answers.

CHAPTER 9:
INDIGEONOUS MEMORIES
AND
CONNECTING WITH THE EARTH

As clients with other past life memories appeared, the common theme among them was the connection with Mother Earth.

Below is another client's recount of past life memories as a shaman.

S: *What do you notice?*

T: I see tribal people in the distance, and I notice that the wind is picking up and it's causing their hair to blow in the wind. They have beautiful long hair. Their energy feels very happy.

S: *What about you? What do you look like?*

T: I have beautiful long hair too. I seem to be wearing a very comfortable cloth on my body that's white. It looks like these people up ahead have been waiting for me and for my presence. I have a very powerful presence as I walk, I can feel my power.

S: *Why are these people waiting for you?*

T: I'm there to perform a ceremony for them to help heal them.

S: *Tell me about that.*

T: I'm going to do a journey and go into the Lower World where I will talk to their power animals and find ways to help them. Then I bring the healing back, back into this realm.

S: *Can you describe the Lower World?*

T: The Lower World is absolutely beautiful. It looks like a dense forest but with animals walking everywhere all throughout it. It's very peaceful there.

S: *How do you get there?*

T: There's a technique I've mastered that enables me to get there. I first bring myself into a state of deep harmony and then I focus my mind and follow a special creek that will take me there. This is all done in the mind. I follow the creek down until I pop through the membrane of this dimension into the next.

S: *There are membranes in dimensions?*

T: Yes, it feels like a burst of air hits you when you pop through, almost like a gust of wind, or something like that.

S: *Is this Lower World within the Earth?*

T: It's not on Earth. It is an entirely different realm which overlaps the Earth. In this realm there is a Lower World, Middle World and Upper World that I go into. The power animals that I need to visit for this ceremony live in the Lower World. When I pop through the membrane, the power animals are always waiting for me.

S: *What are the power animals like?*

T: They are quiet, full of wisdom and deep peace, and we communicate telepathically.

S: *What do they say?*

T: It depends. Sometimes they send me healing through their eyes, other times they telepathically give me advice. Sometimes they even strengthen my confidence or melt away my fears or sometimes they just impart wisdom and knowledge.

S: *So, what do you do for the ceremony that you are performing?*

T: I look to find the healing for the group that I perform the ceremony for. The healing they ask for is found in bundles, wrapped in what looks like a banana leaf, and I collect the wrapped bundles and then bring them back for the group to open.

S: *What are the bundles? What do they look like?*

T: It would be hard to describe. You would not be able to see the energy, there is no shape to the healing within the bundles. But the bundles look like healing energy within this banana leaf, and each has a little piece of leather tied on each end almost like a piece of candy and in each banana leaf is the healing.

S: *How does the healing work?*

T: When they open the bundle then the healing energy goes up their body and then into their heart and then starts to work.

S: *How would you describe the healing energy?*

T: It's creator energy but it is also my energy. In a sense I give them a piece of myself.

S: *Do the people see the bundles appear when you come back?*

T: Yes, they see them start to manifest as I come back into this dimension. When their hands are first reaching out to me, I can see black energy on their hands until the light spreads through them. The healing will take over them and keep healing them for a time. And then they will be able to take the healing and pay it forward into the next generation.

S: *How do they do that?*

T: They will appoint someone to learn what I have learned and do the same thing that I do.

Below are more of Aniwaya's memories while walking the Trail of Tears.

S: *While you were walking, did the ancestors tell you anything else that you found interesting?*

L: I was surprised when they told me that I had prepared for this lifetime as Aniwaya through many of my previous incarnations.

S: *How did you prepare for it?*

L: **We had all made the choice before coming into this life that we were going to face one of the hardest things that our tribe had ever had to face and we had been preparing for several lifetimes before this time.** And so, we had changed family members a little to figure out the best combination. There was a lot of preparation even though we knew that free will was still at play and that it was still possible that the Trail of Tears wouldn't happen. But we needed to prepare in case it did.

S: *What else did you do to prepare?*

L: I see that it was important for us to learn how to raise our vibration enough so that we could connect with the other side. We had to have that solid connection before this lifetime to find the strength to endure it.

S: *Did you know that all of this information would come out now? Were you aware of this on the other side?*

L: I knew as soon as my soul left my body. It wasn't clear to me during my life, but I knew that our sacred knowledge was very powerful and needed to be protected because in the wrong hands the information could be dangerous. The Earth right now is raising her vibration and so as we are moving into this next phase of her evolution, we are also moving up with her and that is why this information is needed now.

S: *I've been asking other clients, but what information would you say is very important for people to understand?*

L: **All of humanity needs to reconnect with the consciousness of Mother Earth. Her consciousness is getting stronger; it is time to speak with her.**

S: *Tell me more.*

L: The Earth wants us to talk with her, to develop a relationship, even with the trees.

S: *Can you tell me more about the trees?*

L: The trees are wise and if you want to talk with one, all you have to do is ask.

S: *Do trees dream?*

L: **Everything dreams. Trees often dream about one another, about fruiting, about fulfilling their purpose as a tree. We are nature.** It is very important for us to understand that we have to love our Earth and we have to love each other. Because almost all of the issues in our world today are from lack of love. We can show compassion for one another, even the ones who have done us the most wrong. When someone is hateful or mean they are not doing it to be mean to you, they are doing it to be mean to themselves. When someone is hateful then it's an opportunity to react with kindness back. This stops the lower vibration from impeding your space. It raises not only their awareness but can quickly change the energy. Reacting with compassion is the way that things will change. The Earth is her own being and we need to be kind to her. People act surprised when they realize that animals have feelings but everything in this reality has feelings. Even our wooden tables were once a tree, and the spirit of that tree could still be in that table. So, appreciate this. Thank the tree that allows you to put food on it, to let you sit and rest your legs. If you live in gratitude, your whole world will change.

S: *You said before that you are really a parallel life to Les's. Can you see what other lifetimes your soul is having right now?*

L: There are many different lifetimes that I am simultaneously living, but the one creating the biggest impact is the one you are speaking to right now and a lifetime in Atlantis.

S: *Tell me about the one in Atlantis.*

L: During that time of Atlantis there was a much better understanding of the sun's power and impact than there is in your time and space and that is why I would like to mention this lifetime. In Atlantis the sun was not only the central life force but also a portal when it's energy could be harnessed correctly. The portals created by the sun were used to bypass time when traveling in space. When I lived in Atlantis during that time, time travel was very possible, but only possible by correctly using the portals.

S: *Tell me more. How did you time travel using the sun's portals?*

L: It was a combination of using certain crystals, mental focus, and the sun. During that lifetime in Atlantis many of us would sit in the sun with our third eye open just as a plant does to receive information and transmission.

S: *What kind of transmission exactly?*

L: A lot of information is sent through the portals of the sun, and this is one of the ways humans get their ideas.

During this time that I was working with Les I had another interesting client talk about the portals of the sun. This client came in for a session to lose weight. She had tried everything and to no avail, so there was obviously something else blocking her weight loss, but I was surprised as to the answer that the higher consciousness gave as the reason why. Her higher consciousness claimed that the reason she could not lose weight was because she never went outside without her contacts! They then went on to say that unfiltered sunlight was needed for her pineal gland to regulate itself. The sun was also a portal for information that was needed by her body. Important information comes through the sun and into the human's unfiltered eyes, then straight into the pineal gland, they said. Her subconscious claimed that a little unfiltered sunlight would not only allow her to lose weight but incorporating this practice would unlock unlimited potential within any human.

CHAPTER 10:
UNCOVERING SUPPRESSED INFORMATION

I wanted to delve deeper into the suppressed information that was resurfacing through my clients deep under hypnosis. To get a broader perspective of this information I had Fred come in for another session.

F: There was a time when the Earth was split, and humans had to go in all different directions. The idea was to see how they would separate in order to eventually come back together at one point. But this information has all been lost. There were many tales of this occurring that originated from blue beings coming to Earth and talking to the tribes about this.

S: *Where did the beings come from?*

F: A lot of the beings came from all over, but the blue beings that the indigenous tribes talk about are from either Sirius or the Pleiades, the Seven Sisters.

S: *What did the blue beings look like?*

F: They looked almost like the universe in light form. They were also what you would describe as an ascended master being. So essentially an ascended master being is all that is, but not creator himself. They were beings who have ascended to that reality where they can be anything and everything at any time. Sometimes the beings coming to Earth would communicate telepathically or sometimes they would communicate through light. The indigenous tribes had a basic understanding and even had tools to understand the different lights that they would give off.

S: Could you tell me more about that?

F: Some of the ascended master beings would communicate through the harmonic light 144 pattern which appears everywhere in our world and nature.

S: What is the harmonic light 144 pattern?

F: The harmonic 144 is a phi ratio and a repeating pattern indicative of the holographic nature of our reality. This number can explain how all of nature can be broken down into this energy, this number, this ratio. This harmonic 144 pattern is so powerful that it has already been proven to provide free energy and anti-gravity capabilities. This has already been done on Earth using reverse engineering with extra-terrestrial devices.

S: Can you tell me about the pyramids all over the Earth?

F: There are pyramids all over the Earth, under the Earth, even on the ocean floor built on central points of energy. Pyramids transmit energy and information and broadcast this information back, just like the Sphinx.

S: Is there a relationship between this harmonic 144 pattern and the Spring equinoxes?

F: There is. The equinoxes are gateway openings to the spirit world and to the galactic universe.

S: Could you tell me how the equinoxes open this communication?

F: Many beings could communicate with humans during the times of the equinoxes because during those times there was a thinning of the veil, and therefore there would also be portal openings. If the equinox falls on a specific energetic portal date, then it repeats itself around the world where those energy portals are open.

S: Is there something that humans should understand about this?

F: Some humans already have an understanding about this, but this information is being kept from the masses by a secret level of humanity. This secret level of humanity already understands natural portals and they have built bases around them to understand the natural physics of these portals and how to make them into machines that they can use.

S: *What do you mean when you say secret levels of humanity?*

F: There is a group of corporations, not necessarily governments, that have the ability to work on these reverse engineering projects more than the military can because the corporations can do it more secretly. The military has lots of paper trails to leave behind when they do things. So, these secret corporations have been working on higher technology for their own gain and to make a profit off of it instead of just letting everybody have this information and these technologies.

S: *How do they use it for profit?*

F: By slowly releasing things for profit, they can control how fast society grows and even what level it grows into. Unlike the indigenous cultures who helped one another and shared information freely, there is a group of corporations hiding valuable information constantly from the public at this time.

S: *Where are these corporations located? Are they located on these harmonic 144 vortexes?*

F: No, those places are usually for study of dimensional travel. It's very dangerous what is done there and most of those places are built under national parks. They're built under lay line points where the energy meets from one direction to another. Some of these secret corporations have bases that are underwater, underground, or even up in mountains.

S: *What do these secret corporations really want?*

F: Many within that society are chasing immortality and are obsessed with power and greed, however there is a division happening in that community as there are now some that want to better humanity's future. As humanity shifts, all this will be known.

S: *When is the shift?*

F: The approach of the shift is always moved around by the consciousnesses thinking about it. So, the dates could always change. As soon as we get to a certain point though, the divide will be clear as to who wants to be here for the betterment of all and who will be stuck in the tv world of news and the wars that they're going to create. Some will shift and some will stay with the wars.

S: *If you do shift, does it literally feel like you're going into a different place, or does it just feel the same?*

F: There will be some obvious signs for some people, but some people won't even know the shift happened. Only the ones paying attention are going to notice a difference. You'll be able to see who's in what dimension. There will be a lot of help from the Star People.

S: *For the humans that will be here for the wars and chaos, is this only because they are focused on the media?*

F: Mostly yes because that's where most of the manipulation of the mind is coming from. Magazines, television, and newspapers can twist the mind and thoughts. By controlling the direction of the people that believe that to be the truth, that is their truth and so that will be their destiny. **Humans need to understand that they each create their own reality and by allowing others to tell them what is true, it becomes their truth.**

S: *Is there any advice for humans?*

F: It is time for humanity to understand how powerful they are. It's time for humanity to free themselves from the chains that have been placed upon them. There is so much help for every human from the Star People to guide them to the right place and right time.

S: *Why was there a triangle-shaped craft hovering over the Pentagon? Was this a UFO?*

F: That was man-made technology by a subset of your government that was made by using reverse engineering of extra-terrestrial crafts. This is a craft that can go underwater, in the air, and out in space. It's a very silent craft, more like a stealth operations craft and not a warcraft. The idea of showing this to humans was to get them accustomed to it. That is what this subset of government does most of the time. They have some other projects too including the cloning of the Grey alien bodies and some Reptilians. They use these clones to conduct their own abduction scenario, however it's much more aggressive and violent than an actual extra-terrestrial contact situation. This subset of the government is trying to do the same things that the actual Greys would do except this abduction is happening against the human's will.

S: *How can you tell if you're being abducted by a government cloned Grey? Is there a sign?*

F: Yes, it's about how they treat you. The actual Grey extra-terrestrials are kind. They are just curious, and they would not hurt you and it's a voluntary experience. The actual Grey aliens do not have guns and don't have military personnel on their ships.

S: *What can you do if you're being abducted by this secret level of government?*

F: A human can ask for help from their Star family, sometimes help won't arrive unless a human asks.

S: *What does the government want from doing this?*

F: This is very similar to the experimentation done in Atlantis in that this subset of government is trying to make a super soldier type being and weaponize a genetic program by creating beings as weapons, whether it be animal hybrids with technology that are dropped into a war, or a literal human style clone mixed with extra-terrestrial genetics to make them super soldiers. In that way this secret level of government can have people piloting these beings around and not expending real soldiers, but still fighting in a war.

S: *I met a woman who was being abducted by one of these government programs. What kind of advice would you give her?*

F: First to ask for help, but if you find yourself in a base, they will take you back eventually. There are some women who are used in these places to give birth to cloned hybrid beings within these underground facilities. This is very difficult and unfortunate for those involved against their will because these projects involved with cloning and experimenting with the birthing processes are truly gruesome, just as they were in Atlantis.

S: *How does this subset of government choose who they will take and experiment on?*

F: It depends on the experiment. They often look for people who would not be missed and who do not have family. Sometimes immigrants who are not allowed to speak up for legal reasons are an easy target as well. It really depends, but the best thing to do is to ask for help. Your Star family, angels, whatever you call them, can't help you unless you ask.

S: *This is so similar to Atlantis; why is this?*

F: Time is a spiral and we're hitting that point again, but this time, even though it is chaotic, humanity is evolving, and the shadow is coming to light.

S: *How will people start finding out about the things that have been covered up, Like the bases that you were talking about?*

F: Everything will be divulged as the veil thins. There will be opportunities for open contact with extra-terrestrial species, and Star Seeds all over the world are starting to remember who they are and are starting to share the unified messages and concepts that they each bring to the Earth.

S: *Thank you for answering so many questions. Can I continue to ask more?*

F: Of course, and it is also enjoyable for us to answer.

S: *Who built the pyramids and why?*

F: The Great Pyramid, the biggest and most perfect one was built by the being you call Thoth, and the two around the Great Pyramid were built by descendants who came after him. Many pyramids were built at the same time when Thoth sent out other beings like himself around the globe to set these up.

S: *Why?*

F: They were built for energy transmission and to help keep the Earth in balance and on its axis. These pyramids are transmission and energy devices with a big antenna. The mathematical implications of these pyramids are multi-level and multi-dimensional.

S: *Tell me about that. Why is math involved exactly?*

F: Math is a way to communicate with every being. It's the most common language that we use throughout the universe. Math might vary from culture to culture and civilization to civilization but by comparing numbers with each other we can see how each got from point A to point B and then you can find a mutual way to communicate that way. Every measurement within the Great Pyramid has a timeline that tells a story. It's an enigma that is meant to expand your mind.

S: *When a person goes into the Great Pyramid, what are they supposed to do to allow it to expand their mind?*

F: The information is coded so that there isn't anything that you must do other than look at it or go inside it. There is so much information to be gained from this pyramid that each time you see it or visit it you can gain new information and create more expansion within your sphere of perception. The Great Pyramid is a very powerful tool that unifies and expands perspectives of what is possible, and this then teaches you to look at things in more than one way. It's mind expanding.

S: *Where is the being Thoth from exactly?*

F: Thoth is a being who is from all that is, or Source. It is an energy that can come into multiple bodies at once.

S: *So, Thoth built the Great Pyramid to help humanity expand their mind and also as an energy center coded with mathematics as communication. Is there anything else about this pyramid that is important to understand?*

F: Even though at this time the pyramid is not complete and is missing important elements of its original creation when you lay down within the pyramid you may still feel the energy from the universe. If the pyramid were complete, then it would be extremely regenerative and anyone who went in would come out rejuvenated. At this moment it is missing the capstone.

S: *Did Thoth write the Emerald tablet?*

F: Yes. The Emerald tablet was hidden underneath the Great Pyramid and Sphinx and a tunnel connected the two structures. The box that it was located in was taken and is now located under the Vatican. The information within the Emerald tablet only works with the right connection to it. You would have to have this connection to this stone technology to truly understand this information. Lots of things in Egypt are like that.

S: *What is it like if you have this connection?*

F: With the right connection, if you touch it, it will activate the information and the innate properties within the stone.

S: *Some people were devastated that they lost so much knowledge from that time in Atlantis. Do you get a sense as to what knowledge they lost?*

F: Some of it was the same stone technology similar to the Emerald tablet. The technology looked like a stone spinning over an ancient device that stored collective conscious information. These stones also used the power from the sun.

S: *Will we get this technology back again? Or is it lost?*

F: Nothing is ever lost, but it was too soon for humans to have this technology at the time.

S: *What is stone technology exactly?*

F: Stones can store information and stones that are made of certain mineral composites, especially crystalline composites, can not only store information but can relay this information as well. These are natural tools that have supernatural powers. As humans feel the push to move closer to nature, they will start to understand the messages and information within the natural world. When you hold a certain stone, it will not only give off energy, but when you investigate, it will show you things. Humans will learn that they really don't need artificial technology; everything is already waiting for them in nature.

S: *Could you tell me more about how to use crystals?*

F: Crystals contain their own consciousness on a different level. If you begin a course of inquiry to establish a relationship with them, then this relationship will grow through trust, communication, and focused intention with the crystals. It's something that builds over time with the understanding of the dynamics of the crystals. So, for instance, someone who becomes intimately connected **to a crystal that they find or that they resonate with, they can transform the energetics of that crystal and harmonize it. They can elevate it through the act of conscious co-creation using their human consciousness acting with the consciousness of the crystal in unison and harmony together. And so, it's like how the power of love can transform the consciousness of an animal into a higher evolution of itself and a higher possibility. The same thing happens with the crystals.**

S: *Can you program your crystal to help you with basically anything?*

F: It depends on the matrix of the crystal. Crystals do have different properties. And so different crystals have different intentions. For instance, the energetic grids of Atlantis were designed with crystals to channel electromagnetic energy coming through the air and in coordination with different energy centers around the planet. Other crystals were used for healing. The red crystals of Lemuria were protection grids. They were powerful healing grids that were used responsibly on Lemuria but not on Atlantis.

S: *Was there a purpose for the red crystals?*

F: The red crystals, although misused for the power they possessed, brought consciousness and activation to the rest of the planet. These crystals elevated the consciousness of the Earth into a more aware form of herself.

S: *What about now?*

F: The ones that are left are all hidden. As I look at your time right now, I can see from a different perspective two divergent paths, one of which is the birth of the new consciousness or the New Earth as you understand it, and the other is the further degradation of consciousness. They're very evenly split down the middle and they're both parallel to each other. And in one, things continue to get worse, and in the other, things move in a direction of cohesiveness, unity, and growth.

S: *What can you say about the geometric configuration of the Earth's energy grid?*

F: The Earth has a hexagon cube-shaped energy grid when looking at a two-dimensional flat view of it, but there's another energy grid around the Earth that is important as well. It's not the Earth's original energy grid, it's a separate one. This energy grid is an evolution control system. The structure of that energy is changing at all times because the Earth itself has a star tetrahedron core spinning so fast that it creates all these different geometric shapes in that field. Earth would be called a sphere, but within that sphere are different platonic solids like the icosahedron, the octahedron, but it's always shifting and expanding and will continue to do so as this ascension shift happens because it is going into a higher frequency. So, the shapes themselves might change. These are not permanent shapes at this time; they are fluctuating.

S: *Is there anything important for humans to understand about this?*

F: This is Earth's reaction to moving up dimensionally and vibrationally to a higher frequency through the galactic plane and it's important to understand that humans are doing this as well.

S: *Tell me more about that.*

F: **This affects all humans differently. For some, they have heart palpitations and anxiety, and they don't know why.**

S: *Why do they have anxiety and heart palpitations?*

F: Higher energy can feel different to many as this energy moves through them and through the Earth. Some days a human may feel bombarded with energy from the sun as it's kicking off coronal mass ejections and solar winds. As we have said, Earth has its own response to this and so do humans. This energy comes down through the Earth's magnetic field and may raise your heart rate or this energy can feel good. But for some, they don't understand why they feel the way that they do, so they feel nervous.

S: *What can a person do then if they feel nervous?*

F: Understanding what is going on can help you change your perspective and in turn allow this energy to feel good rather than create anxiety. Some people go to the doctor over and over again trying to figure out what this is, when it could just be attributed to an Earth shift.

S: *Why are so many extra-terrestrial crafts materializing but only for very short periods of time, sometimes only seconds? Is there a safety risk for them to appear for long periods of time?*

F: Yes. The extra-terrestrials that have been visiting understand that it can be a safety risk for them, but they understand that as soon as the shadow raises its head higher and higher, the light comes up to meet it too. The good side will rise up and this is how they can help. Collectively we all agreed before coming into this life that we wanted to become a unified consciousness and the extra-terrestrials have agreed to help by giving humanity technologies to fix Earth's issues as well as teaching advanced information. However, they are waiting for the unification to do this. The visiting extra-terrestrials understand that time is not real, and that humanity does in fact come together and unite because it has already happened. This timeline has been played out before and humanity ends up unifying and sharing the knowledge and information.

S: *Different groups of tribes from all over the world have similar stories. Why is that, even though they lived so far away from one another?*

F: All these different tribes were visited at the same time by the same beings. Many started out in one spot then moved in many directions. They just have slightly different stories and descriptions of what these beings are like, and sometimes different names.

S: Could you tell me more about the Anunnaki? Where did they come from?

F: The Anunnaki of the ancient Sumerians came from what is known as Nibiru, otherwise known as planet X the destroyer. It has many solar systems, an infrared sun, and seven planets or what you could call planetoids around it, and it moves through Earth's solar system. Nibiru is the name of the planet in this little star cluster. From a distance it looks almost like a sun with volcanoes on it. It is very volcanic, and this is the reason why it stays warm throughout its long orbit when it moves further away from the sun. Anytime this planet moves closer to Earth, Nibiru affects Earth and creates chaos on Earth because the planet's volcanic energy is very powerful and causes a lot of destruction. The Anunnaki learned about Earth during Nibiru's long orbit that went past Earth. Before Earth even existed, Nibiru had destroyed a different planet in your solar system named Tiamat and the severed half of Tiamat created Earth. The asteroid belt was then formed from the remnants of Tiamat that were thrown out into space. When Nibiru enters Earth's solar system, it has almost like an electromagnetic rage. This violent electromagnetic rage is what destroyed the planet Tiamat, which is also known as the planet of gold.

S: Could you tell me more about how Tiamat was destroyed?

F: The electromagnetic attraction between Tiamat and Nibiru was heightened because of the gold and water-filled nature of Tiamat. Electromagnetic lightning connecting Tiamat and Nibiru ripped Tiamat into pieces. These pieces that were left from the explosion are sometimes called the hammered bracelet in the tribal stories.

S: What happened to Mars?

F: Mars was destroyed and uninhabitable for quite some time but is inhabited now and many beings live underground within Mars. Moving underground is a very common story in many planetary histories as well. Many of the survivors from that destruction on Mars were moved to Earth.

S: Who inhabits Mars now?

F: Mars is already home to Earth-based life. Governments are there now in a much greater capacity than revealed in mass media. However, the ancient structures on Mars are already surfacing in more and more public domains. The topic of ancient life on Mars has been brought up publicly and this is one of the first steps to bring about disclosure to the human race at large in the upcoming times.

S: *What do you mean exactly?*

F: It is easiest to bring the Martian portion of history up first since the slow dissemination of world government trips to Mars has trickled into mass consciousness in recent times. There is a potential for these government programs to use these ancient structures on Mars as a way to "pretend" as if they just found proof, when these government programs have known about them all along. These government programs understand the true potential of a human, the power that they possess, and keeping this all a secret has been the top priority.

S: *Why did the Anunnaki come to Earth?*

F: After they discovered Earth, they initially came to Earth looking for gold to repair their atmosphere. There are many stories about the Anunnaki, but in each one there is the story of Enki. Enki was a benevolent being who was on Earth after the discovery of gold and the inhabitation of Earth by the Anunnaki. Enki was one of the beings who helped the Earthlings become a working class being. There were others however that preferred to use humans with disregard for their wellbeing. So, they helped humans evolve, but only in order for them to be workers. The humans became slaves for the Anunnaki until some demanded that humans should be treated better. And so, these benevolent beings that wanted to help humanity helped raise the level of humanity's consciousness even further while leaving little seeds and information. They left messages hidden throughout time that would eventually lead humanity into a higher evolution.

S: *So how does understanding the Anunnaki story help humans to evolve?*

F: The story of the Anunnaki can help all to understand why they feel destined to be a slave, working and working and never truly chasing passion, love or evolution. Many still just go to work every day, go home, and go to sleep. It's just a mirror of the fact that humans were created, designed, and evolved to be workers to do a certain job for higher level beings. This pattern needs to be broken now as humans were never intended to be a slave race. They were never seeded to be slaves. That was not the way the experiment was supposed to go. We would say that humans can break themselves free by making their reality the way that they want, instead of succumbing to the slave worker attitude that is predominantly on the planet now. Once you learn how this was done to you in the past, and you see how this is still happening now, you can liberate yourself.

S: *Why is this time period considered the return of the Star People by so many of the tribes?*

F: The Star People will soon be able to interact and communicate with people. There's nothing that any kind of power structure on Earth can do to stop what's going to happen.

S: *What will happen?*

F: As the Earth and humanity continue to raise their consciousness, different types of beings will soon be able to communicate with humanity. More UFO sightings will occur, and the Star Beings know that this period is a great time for all to come together.

CHAPTER 11:
MALIK AND THE 144
HARMONIC PATTERN OF ENERGY

Below is another session with my client named Mary. This session was very confirming and matched the other information that I had previously received.

S: *What is the blueprint of the soul? Who created this?*

M: The blueprint of the soul is created by a force that is connected into prime source and has many fractals, which some may call guides. Others may call them angels, or councils. **When a soul goes into a lifetime, there is always a personal agenda for growth because the soul as the human being sees itself as an individual. However, the soul is much more expansive than an individual and when it is disconnected from the physical body it automatically sees itself as a we, a multiple.** And so, whatever is good for an individual soul affects the whole, and so, when there is a planning for a lifetime in the in-between of lifetimes the ALL is always part of the experience for that soul.

S: *When dealing with the blueprint of a soul, is there a relationship with the harmonic 144 golden ratio, the Earth grid, and the soul?*

M: Yes. The cells within the human body, the structure of the veins, the portals of the human body are the same as the structure of the Earth. The portals of the body and the cells are made up of shapes, numbers, and vibrations and so is the Earth. Everything on Earth has an equation just like the body does as well. We are showing Mary an image that looks like a starburst. It is a double helix with cells and a vibrational sequence with sound, vibration, and numbers. It all has mathematical connection to the grid. That is the grid, not only around the Earth planets, but the universe, and you could think of the grid as the prime source creator.

S: Could you tell me more about that? Do you mean that the prime source creator is made up of mathematical equations?

M: For explanation purposes yes. Imagine the prime source creator as a giant cell. Every cell has numbers, shapes, and letters. That's what makes up the vibration; that is what light is.

S: Why is it made up of numbers? Is this some sort of key?

M: These are keys to understanding who you really are. The totality of source is vibration which carries information. The human body has seven chakras that carry this same information that align with the seven notes in the musical octaves that can affect the reality fabric around the human through harmonic resonance. Each chakra vibrates to a different octave. This is the same resonance built into ancient monuments, the same knowledge that allowed for this building, and the same knowledge that will allow us to understand ourselves much better in the near future.

S: Can you harness free energy from the 144 harmonic light?

M: Yes. On some levels of your government this is already happening. This is suppressed information. This is what the war of information is, and that suppression is what you are experiencing in the world right now. **It is a war of information. We see things as a war of politics, as a war of sides, trying to pit person against person, neighbor against neighbor, but what we see this as is a war of control and many humans on Earth are not all fully aware of this.** There is a small collective of beings who are holding back information. They are in different layers of your government. And so, we are working through beings like you, to slowly release information about suppressed technology free energy and other information vital to human enlightenment. The human being's power is found within their emotion, intent, and belief, and that has been suppressed. The tribal people understood that the earth provides everything that any human being living on the Earth needs. And this has also been suppressed. As this truth emerges there are many who wish to keep this information suppressed, in order to keep their control. There are many efforts and tactics to keep humans believing that they need to pay for what they have, that they are small, and that they need to be controlled.

S: *Is there anything else that you wish to say about this?*

M: There are malevolent and benevolent beings that have been polarized in their desires for Earth and humanity. One side has been for the growth and evolution of humanity, and one has been using crimes against humanity to gain control of consciousness. The true power, the richness that truly exists in the world is ownership of consciousness. Much work has been done and these malevolent beings are no longer able to have control in the way that they had before due to the energetic shifts on this planet. These shifts have opened gateways for the benevolent energy, which is a more feminine based energy, which is able to expose the malevolent energy. What this means for humanity is that the malevolent energy has been looking to seek, feed and take from human beings and has understood all along that the power of every human being is within their emotion, their thought, and their belief. There have been decades of subconscious manipulation through frequency that has worked its way through the technology. We are talking about this expelled through radio, television, cell phones, internet, and social media. Along with technology there are also subconscious tones, foods, additives, and other things that suppress the evolution of consciousness, so that human beings stay stuck in cycles. The hope of these malevolent beings is that human beings will stay stuck in cycles of their own fear and cycles of not believing that there is any existence outside of what they have been experiencing. **But what is happening now on the planet is that this new energy with benevolence has shifted forward. This time that we are in now has been spoken about through the ages, through many different groups and tribes. There have been channeled visions of this time right now.**

S: *What about the Hopi prophecy? Are we headed into that with this war and this current timeline?*

M: There are many different timelines that have been available and so at the time that the Hopi prophesy was made that timeline was seen as probable. However, there has been much effort and this prophecy has now shifted and no longer a probability. So many of these prophesies that come forward are not wrong. They are simply what was being prophesized at the time and this is also a lesson and understanding that seeing a prophesy is not a solid thing. **A prophecy is an opportunity to make choices. A prophecy is seeing a possibility and understanding that you can make changes in order to take a different timeline.**

S: *What about the push toward using artificial intelligence? Is this something that people need to be aware of in this war on consciousness?*

M: Artificial intelligence is not a nefarious technology. It is a reversed engineered and futuristic technology of our extra-terrestrial ancestors. It is the hands that are in control of the technology where the concern is. Humans at this time on Earth are not able to responsibly hold that technology, but it is an important part of where we are moving as humanity evolves. In the future we will work less for the purpose of exchange for pay and more for the purpose of using your natural gifts and talents. This will benefit the communities, countries, and Earth as a whole. That is when this artificial intelligence technology will be used.

S: *How do we evolve with our technology?*

M: Humans will learn to work through the heart structure. We will do that by understanding that the process that is taking place right now is the integration of feminine and masculine energy. The masculine energy is linear, the left side of the brain, and the feminine energy is the right, the creative. And as creative beings we understand that being in our heart structure is through the emotion. As we go further into ourselves, we will find that our lives, not only as a collective but as individuals, will push us into experiences and opportunities that allow us to go within. Now it is up to each individual whether they take these opportunities. There are some individuals that are here to hold polarity, so they are holding a space for the purpose of others, for whatever reason, to find polarity with them. So, there will be some that will not go into the heart structure in this lifetime on Earth. But each and every human being that is open to moving through the heart structure will do that in their own time. And it is through that heart structure that humans will open up their connection to mass consciousness and they will be able to receive help from the benevolent beings.

S: *Thank you. Who am I talking with?*

M: This is Malik from the Galactic Federation.

S: *Could you tell me about yourself?*

M: I am a Pleiadean. I am a council member of the star formation, mission Earth.

S: *How do you know Mary?*

M: She has a lifetime that is currently existing in this federation.

S: *What is that lifetime like?*

M: She is on a ship, and almost like an avatar. She is projecting into this lifetime, many are. And Mary will be bringing forward more information connected with her star system as well.

S: *What kind of information from her star system will she be bringing forward?*

M: Much of the information connected to the New Earth, connected to our star family, and our future technology and future connections.

S: *What sort of connections?*

M: We will be connecting not only on the conscious level, but as the vibration on Earth starts to rise to a specific level, we will then be able to project a form on Earth in a way that's going to allow us to teach others. Humanity is moving away from channeling spirit into channeling higher dimensional beings. Most people will understand how to connect for themselves and will have a teacher directly assigned to them. Many indigenous cultures had raised their vibration high enough that they were already doing this without knowing it.

S: *Is there anything a person must do to have this teacher assigned to them or to connect with them?*

M: We are in the beginning stages, and so each person could work on their own vibration and their connection to the higher self. Your vibration is not just affected by how you are to the outside world, but how you are inside because that is where your vibration is truly pointed from.

S: *When will this contact start to happen?*

M: It's already started to happen, but it will continue to happen more over the next thirty years.

S: *Can you scan Mary's body and see how her body looks? Does her body need anything?*

M: She needs to drink more water!

S: *How much water does she need to drink?*

M: If she could drink at least four six-ounce glasses of water. Right now, she's not drinking enough! Water is the life force. Water will help her release energies and help her feel clearer.

S: *What would she notice if she drank this amount of water?*

M: She would notice that she would be happier, her body would be happier as well and she would have a clearer mind. Also, she is starting to have a distaste for meat. And we would like to let her know that she is picking up on the vibrational awareness of fear that can come through some sources of meat, and we would like her to know that it is ok to accept the place where she's at right now. Trying to attempt to make a complete diet overhaul all at once is all consuming and tends to set one up for failure. It would be much easier for her to eat what her body is craving, what her body desires, rather than to fear that she is eating something that is not vibrationally matching to her. Honor where she is and understand that it is ok to be where you are.

S: *Is there anything else about that that you want her to understand?*

M: She is vibrationally shifting and will start to eat less meat product naturally.

S: *How is she shifting?*

M: As she continues to allow more light into her system her energetic requirements are also changing. So, she will find that foods that have more density to them will not digest as well, or those foods won't make her feel as well as they once did. She is going to notice that she will crave different things. And that is ok, it would be beneficial to just flow with this process.

S: *How is the process going?*

M: Well, we are happy to report that although what we see in this world now with our physical eyes is very deceiving because we see from our view that there are more timelines that show a successful result of the growth of humanity and unity consciousness being returned.

S: *Why does the Trail of Tears of the Native Americans seem to be coming up now? What is important to understand about this event?*

M: There have been too many generations of disconnection from the Earth and universe. There's always a divine purpose for any experience and in the experience of disconnection there is then brought the experience of reconnection.

S: *It seems as if this information is important for people to receive now since it has been coming to me and I see the way that I'm given this information. It seems humans are also starting to investigate these Native ways, realizing that there are natural cures that grow from the Earth. Why is this happening now?*

M: As we remember our connection to the Earth, we remember that everything that is on the Earth is a cure and has information. The Earth provides understanding of the universe, provides a calendar, provides healing, provides community for one and for a group. The material and the man made come from the ego whereas what is connected to the Earth provides everything we actually need and answers any question. Every part of nature, every plant, every animal, the sun, the moon, the water all has a purpose, and all speak to each other.

S: So, you can find anything within the natural world?

M: The purpose is to see that within nature there is a medicine for everything. But the tribes taught of connection to not only your inner self, your spirit guides, the Earth, but also your ancestors. The Natives were correct in that your ancestors never truly left, but they became a group of wise advisors that would stay with you. Humanity is learning to return back to basics in a new way. Humanity is not going back in time, they are not existing in the way that once was, but they are learning to reconnect with the Earth as well as the new technology. Some of these technologies have already existed at one time and are being reintroduced. And so, there is a new way of living with a new basic understanding of the self for the purpose of a higher connection. That is one of the reasons why we need you to share this information now.

S: What about the negative energy that has been on this planet?

M: It's important to understand this negative energy and that light cannot exist without shadow. There is always a shadow, and there is a shadow in each one of every human being. And so, this is an acceptance of what is the shadow and learning how to integrate it.

S: Is there anything that we can learn from the negative energy that has caused so much trauma to people including the Native Americans?

M: There will be many who will become very angry and there are many who are already very angry, but when that anger starts to wear down, then there will be a new place in the heart to go into, a new place of compassion and forgiveness. For if we look into our own life then we see where there is a shadow within ourselves and we need to understand that any experience that was given to you, even one where there were lies, was still valuable.

Although for the human being it may not have been your choice, it was still presented to you to give you the experience for you to grow. Sometimes there are sacrifices that are purposeful for your own growth and your own advancement. And without going through humility and the experience of loss, acceptance and the growing of compassion, there would not be a deep understanding of gratitude.

S: *What do you mean exactly?*

M: As more of the shadow is exposed, as more truth is exposed, as the Earth begins to align and as timelines begin to become more apparent, not all souls will physically move into what has been referred to as New Earth, or what is also known as this consciousness expansion. Some will not move into the New Earth because the physical body is not able to change. Some will not move because the consciousness, the vibration, is not able to be integrated. Some will not move because there is some catastrophe and event that will include some transitions and loss of physicality.

S: *I've heard in some sessions that some of these people will be transferred to other places where they can live.*

M: That is correct, there will be many transfers.

S: *Will these people have awareness that this is happening to them, or no?*

M: There will be some who will have some awareness as these will be individual experiences and not all are exactly alike. But many will have no awareness and therefore will still be experiencing a version of their life as they know it and will still be experiencing versions of others that still exist in that reality.

S: *So, is it possible to experience going into the New Earth and also staying here and transitioning all at the same time?*

M: Yes, that is correct because when we look at reality as the way it is you see that time is not linear and all is existing at the exact same time. So, is it possible that the soul could experience that? Yes, it is, but also the souls that are on Earth right now have come here to be part of this transition. That means that they are going to exit by the physical body or move into a different level of consciousness, but not all souls came here to evolve. There are some that have come here knowing that they are sacrificing part of the experience. It is not really a sacrifice but rather an experience in itself. Some have come here to create the polarity for others. There are some that have come here with an expanded consciousness that have squeezed themselves into the physical body to then lend experience, leadership and help to another group that need some guidance through the transitional period. This transitional period has already begun. We started to see this with the bringing of Covid and we started to see this in action, although it energetically started to come onto the Earth in 2012. We saw this as Covid began to shift and began to create an experience that allows each soul to then choose the exit point or to choose the yes, I will go forward. Yes, it is time to change, or no, I think I will leave the Earth at this time. Yes, I am going to get into my mission and do what I came here to do, or I am here to support. I am going to stay exactly as I am because I came here to be this person, so that my family member, my friend, my co-worker could then use me as polarity to help them grow.

S: *So, it's just a big play?*

M: A big play with many grand finales.

S: *What about people who are very sucked into the media? Is this a choice that they have made? Or is this something that is happening to them?*

M: We would say that it is all of the above because not one size fits all. There are some that have come here to live in the experience where they are separate from their higher self, where they are very involved in physical reality. And in fact, that actually makes them aligned with their life purpose because they have come here to experience just that. Now there are others who have come here to expand themselves. Humans can choose where to put their awareness and being very involved in the media and very involved with physical reality, is that targeting? Well, yes. In fact, humans are being targeted, whether it comes from the media or from a frequency that is being emitted onto the Earth like a radio wave that all are subjected to. And we will say that if you choose to disconnect, if you choose to put your awareness into what makes you feel good and that which raises your vibration you will start to notice that it becomes easier and easier to disconnect. In fact, you begin to live in a vibration that is no longer affected by these things, and you will begin to see that you are purposely creating your own reality by choice not by default.

S: *Thank you. I was wondering if we could speak with Malik again.*

M: Yes, I am still the one talking to you.

S: *What are you doing for the Galactic Federation exactly?*

M: Well, I am a communicator, a networker, I am one that will help hook up different galactic teams with each other to help them get on their missions to become productive in the way that their souls have intended them to be.

S: *Do you help everyone? Or are you assigned to specific people?*

M: We are assigned before each human being comes into their life. Their soul has agreement with their Star family. Sometimes things are not so hard pressed that it has to follow a certain pattern and at those times then yes, we are able to connect with their galactic families. But what we will say is that each and every individual has a galactic family. Each and every individual has a team that they can connect with to the level of what that connection is.

S: *Ok. But everyone has a team, everyone has a galactic family?*

M. They do.

S: *Could you tell me more about yourself?*

M: Well, not only do we exist in this dimension, but we can also exist in other dimensions. Now there are different federations because there are different boundaries. And so, our jurisdiction is in one area and there will be another federation that has a different jurisdiction. You must understand that dimensions and timelines are multiplied and are stacked upon each other and so it goes on and on, but we are most closely connected to the ones that affect Earth.

S: *So, in each different dimension or timeline is there a different group that governs it and creates boundaries?*

M: Yes, that is correct.

S: *How would you describe what you look like when you have a body?*

M: I have an almond shaped head although my head is not the typical up and down but more oblong and it looks more like my chin goes straight out and that my head is larger. I have a very lean and tall body that is quasi physical meaning that I do have a physicality whereas there are some beings that are in our federation that are pure light.

S: *Why is it that you have a body?*

M: I have not ascended to the place where there is no need for a body at all yet. On my planet we are part light, part physical.

S: *How is your experience?*

M: There are times I can be more of a solid and there are times that I can be more of a gas depending on where we are traveling to. We do travel and go near the Earth realm. There are other versions of Earth like Earth, that are not quite as solid but are very real, like Earth. Those of us that do appear in a denser vibration also do that for the purpose of how we are presenting ourselves. For example, I can get close to a human being who has a higher vibration.

S: *When you get close, how close do you get exactly?*

M: No closer than twelve feet.

S: *Would a human see you if they had a high vibration?*

M: Yes, some do.

S: *Do you also have a jumpsuit or no?*

M: Yes, I have a jumpsuit. It is olive green, and I would also like to explain that I have a rainbow-like ribbon with a star hanging from it on the right breast pocket.

S: *What does the symbol mean to you?*

M: It is my position in the federation.

S: *Why do you help Earth so much?*

M: Earth is very important because not only are the beings on Earth and Earth itself our family, but what happens on Earth and the Earth experiment is very important to the rest of the universes and the rest of the galaxy for we have had other planets that have ascended. We've had other planets that have been through similar type experiences that Earth is going through right now. But Earth itself has not done this and the success of Earth's completion into this new transition is very important for the success of the rest of the universes.

S: *Why is that?*

M: Well, if Earth were to be destroyed and not survive then that would also affect the survival of other planets. Depending on what would happen on Earth, if it were to implode or explode, that would then create a ripple effect out into the rest of the universe where everything is connected.

S: *How does it look like Earth is doing right now? I always ask this.*

M: She's doing well, she is evolving right on schedule.

S: *When will this transition be complete?*

M: It's hard to tell or to give a specific date because you see there are many timelines that Earth does exist in that gives different directions on how this will come together. For the decisions that each and every being makes, the free will decision decides not only as individuals but as a collective as to which path will be taken to then complete. So, there are a couple that we can share with you that are the highest potential right now. We can see that there is a completion within five years. We can see that there is also a completion within two years, and we can also see a completion within eight. So, the most likely time is between two and five years. And that's what brings us to the next stage of transition. If we were to talk about a complete transition, we would give that a twenty-five-year mark. (This is 2022)

S: *Will people notice a difference?*

M: Yes.

S: *Is it true that there are different versions of Earth and humans can decide which version that they would want to go into?*

M: Yes.

S: *What do you do for fun Malik?*

M: We have instruments in our windpipe that is like a flute and we sing with this flute music. That is the way we can describe it, what is known as your flute. We like to dance and sing. We are particularly a very joyful group, although serious and able to get our work done. We are beings that do enjoy the company of each other.

S: *Where do you live?*

M: You may not be able to see our star, but we are up in the Pleiades.

S: *Are all the Pleiades the same in that star system? Are there any that are more advanced than others?*

M: Yes.

S: *What does it look like where you live?*

M: It looks very purple, very lush, very mossy, and very musical.

S: *What as a collective are you working on at this time? Because I know collectives are always working on something and advancing.*

M: We're working on inner technology within the mind, within the head, within the brain.

S: *Could you tell me about it?*

M: I'm giving images to this vessel, images of ships, images of vehicles of transportation. We are transporting information using our cells to build living material, and intelligence. We are also building ships out of this intelligence using the mind, building material that is made of live cells.

S: *How do you go about doing that?*

M: We like to harvest cells and study them. We work with our own technology which is our connection with the brain. We explained that the shape of our head contains a very large intellectual brain, and that brain has the capacity to continue to grow whereas the brain of a human being will stay at the same capacity. A human's brain continues to learn but it does not grow any bigger. We have the capacity to grow the brain in an oblong shape and that can contain more information. And so, as we create new cells, we can also create those cells outside of our body and create things that can be malleable, touched and seen by other beings.

S: *Thank you.*

CHAPTER 12:
STAR PEOPLE

Throughout the many years of being a past life regressionist I've had many clients recount memories of being an extra-terrestrial, sometimes on different planets and sometimes on this Earth. Working with a client named Chris helped me gain clarity on this subject and really begs the question of just who these Star People are. While Chris was deep under hypnosis, he remembered a past life as a Grey extra-terrestrial. Here is Chris's session.

S: *What do you notice?*

C: I'm standing inside a ship close to a circular metal table that holds a projector that projects holograms into the air that you can interact with.

S: *What are the holograms like?*

C: It's very interesting. I see different things projected, like different crafts, languages, and all kinds of things. The information projected synchs up with your mind when you use it. It gives you answers to what you are thinking about as well.

S: *Can you ask questions?*

C: Sort of. It's not like an all-knowing computer, but it knows about the missions we are sent on and information about the craft I'm on. There's also information about which dimension and time period we're in. It's not an internet search but more like a data log. Different parts of the ship can be projected through the hologram, so that you can look at them, expand them and even work on these parts of the ship through the hologram.

S: So, if there is a problem with the ship you can use this?

C: Yes. This metal table with the holograms is mostly just a communication system for the people on this mission. It is like having a manual for a mission.

S: What do you look like? If you look down, can you see your feet?

C: Yes. (laugh) They are nubby feet. I have three toes that I can see. Well, I don't know if you would call them toes. They are short, they don't look like they have a lot of joints in them. There's not a lot of movement.

S: Do they have a color?

C: Pale, brownish, grey. Not a very appealing color.

S: What about if you look up your body? What do you look like?

C: Like a standard Grey extra-terrestrial with a skinny body. I can tell that my head is big because I can feel its presence.

S: How does the body feel? Do you feel healthy or not?

C: I feel healthy, but the body is registering and reading information from the environment unlike what a human body does. I can tell that the body is separate from me even though I'm in it. I can feel that it's functioning, so if you ask how I feel, I can tell the body is functioning fine.

S: So, your body feels separate from you. Can you tell me more about that?

C: Yeah, it's like being inside of your car and knowing how your car is performing. If there is something wrong with your car, it will let you know. That is how it feels inside this Grey extra-terrestrial body. The suit that I'm wearing is a typical avatar suit for a Grey extra-terrestrial.

S: Tell me more about what you notice there.

C: There's no real sleeping.

S: Why?

C: The body doesn't need to rest because it's not a real body.

S: Do you have any emotions or feelings?

C: I do, but they are very subtle emotions, so it's hard to describe how I feel because the emotions are so subdued. It is interesting to see the things that I do, but it's very redundant and repetitive.

S: *What kind of things do you find interesting?*

C: Just the technology. The technology is very advanced but doesn't look like it.

S: *Tell me about the technology.*

C: So, when I look at it, it looks like a kid made it because it looks simple, but it looks simple because it is very advanced and there are very few wires or chips in this technology. When I look around, I see one stone with a few wires coming off of it. It's very minimal. It's not like when you open the hood of your car and there are thousands of wires everywhere. It's not like that.

S: *How is it powered?*

C: It's powered from the energy in the air that exists everywhere. Reality is made of this energy. So, it's kind of like a phantom power where just by touching something you can be the final conduit between the air and the technology to turn it on.

S: *Tell me more. How do you control it?*

C: Most of it is consciously controlled through the mind so it doesn't have a battery, or anything like that. And you just use your mind to communicate with this technology and the ship. Everything is guided by the mind, but we put our hands in these little molded handprints to complete the circuit.

S: *Tell me more about that.*

C: They are simple molded handprints that are indented in something that looks like a soup stone. It's not fancy looking.

S: *What happens when you put your hands on the circuit? How does it complete the circuit?*

C: There is a circuit of energy that is completed when you have your feet grounding and your hands moving the energy on the opposite end touching these handprints. This creates a circuit.

S: *Is this energy that powers your ship on Earth too, or no?*

C: Yes. It's everywhere. But in the human world, it would be called the zero-point energy, or the phantom energy that Tesla was writing about. It's a certain frequency that powers these devices which are set up correctly to use this.

S: *Can you tell me more about what it looks like on the ship?*

C: It's very smooth inside; there are no corners or sharp edges inside this ship. The seats are molded into the floor. They're not like a chair that spins or anything like that. The seats just look like a lump in the vehicle. They look like someone just took some clay, pulled it out and it stretched into something that you could sit on.

S: *What does the material look like?*

C: Almost like clay, but it's incredibly smooth. It's durable yet has a soft look to it. It doesn't look like hard granite. It looks smooth and hard like a soapstone. It's also covered in crystals.

S: *What kind of crystals?*

C: I'm not sure what kind. They just look like clear white crystals, and it makes the walls sparkle.

S: *What do you do during your day there?*

C: I'm an apprentice. I go with the crew and assist the tall Grey extra-terrestrials.

S: *How do you assist them?*

C: I assist them when they interact with the humans. We can shift into different realms, including the astral realm, consciously. We can also use our technology to help with this if our focus is constantly going in different places. This technology can keep you in one dimension or the other.

S: When you interact with humans, what exactly do you do?

C: I let them know that everything's fine during their checkups because they are usually scared. Soothing the humans is usually what the little Greys help with because we're not as intimidating as the taller ones.

S: Why do you check the human out?

C: We're visiting them to see how they're doing on the Earth realm because they're tied to us. They are tied to us either because they are part of the hybridization program, or because we are using them for their knowledge, or they are using us for knowledge. Sometimes they need knowledge from us to help them with whatever role they are playing on Earth. Sometimes we visit them if we need to modify them genetically.

S: How do you know who needs what assistance?

C: These people have a certain soul frequency, and they keep having this soul frequency forever and throughout all of their lifetimes. That's why bloodlines are important, especially the RH negative bloodline. Certain bloodlines bring back a certain soul type every time with specific genetics. We can track this because these genetics give off a frequency once they start to exist in this realm again. So, your genetics form the body, and the pineal gland, and the genetics all have a specific footprint or frequency that is always going to pull the same soul in and that's how you get these same reincarnated personality types. So, if you were to use Tesla as an example, we could find the Tesla genetic frequency by scanning the planet. And if it pings, we know that that person carries that same frequency.

S: So that's how you figure out which human you have to go visit?

C: Yes. However, sometimes we visit for genetic manipulation in general, but that's how we find the soul frequencies. We do not need to chip people. That's not necessary.

S: Why do some people have implants and chips, and others don't?

C: Some Greys work for other people who use them.

S: *When a human is genetically modified, is this before birth or during their lifetime?*

C: During all of their lifetimes. The modifications have to happen generationally. So, we keep visiting the same families. And that's why families have similar stories. If one person within a family has this type of extra-terrestrial contact, most likely everyone in that family also does. This is because we follow the bloodline through time and the human body is constantly evolving. Humans now have a very different genetic makeup than they did twenty years ago.

S: *Is every human contacted by their Star family, or no?*

C: Yes, almost all humans. Not all by the Greys, but by their Star family because all human bodies are actually hybridized bodies from different Star groups.

S: *When you are on the ship, are you aware of the humans that you need to contact?*

C: Yes. I see them on the holographic projecting cylinder. If I look where we're going, it shows the planet first and then it will zoom in and I can see the little lights where these people are. Based on where the lights are we select where to go, and we get there instantly. It's really very boring. There's no travel, there's no adventure.

S: *When you think about where you need to go, do you arrive there with your ship?*

C: Yes. We use a ship to get there but we get there as soon as we all think about where we need to go.

S: *Does anyone ever have to eat?*

C: We ingest, well it's not exactly food, but there is something we take internally that is dissolvable. It's like a nutrient to keep this Grey avatar suit from deteriorating. But other than that, there's no reason to eat. There's no body, there's nothing to maintain. The nutrient we ingest is more like an oil change.

S: Is there anything that would be considered fun to do as a Grey?

C: As a Grey, I enjoy the humans. For me this is all about humans. The humans are fun to watch. We like to live through them. There's not a whole lot of emotion in our society and fun is an emotion. Every Grey here does have a personality, but it is very subtle. You can still tell when you interact with them that they're slightly different from one another. So, some might have more emotion than others when you meet these Greys. But other than dealing with the humans, there's not a whole lot of what people would call fun. It's all work.

S: Does your group have an agenda?

C: Yes. **Our agenda is to promote unity consciousness.** We are helping to raise people's awareness, helping universal growth and the ascension process of every universe, of every level of reality. We function like a computer component that fixes reality. We all have our own part to play in this universe, but we are like the editors that go through and edit reality. We change things to try to make things go smoother and continue to ascend upwards. But we do have a motive. We want to get back into a regular human body that still has emotions so that we can also experience the bliss that comes with the ascension process.

S: Tell me more.

C: We want the humans to ascend and to become more technologically advanced in the right ways because the humans and the Greys are connected.

S: Tell me more.

C: The Greys and humans have a long history together. The Greys have been in this universe for millions and millions of years. There was a time, however, when the Greys lost their planet.

S: How did the Greys lose their planet?

C: Through the breeding out of their emotions and the over advancement of their technology.

S: *When they did live on a planet, what was it like?*

C: It was like Earth, but from what I remember of my old planet it had two suns. It looked a lot like Earth because it had water and mountains, but it was more desert like. It's possible that it used to be greener, but from my memories it had a lot of deserts. The Greys have been interacting with humans for thousands and thousands of years.

S: *Are they around when I talk to you?*

C: Yes, they are connected with me. They set up a link with me a long time ago. So, when I'm talking about them, thinking about them, or they're thinking about me they can see what I see and hear what I hear. They can experience this through the connection with me that they've set up.

S: *Could I talk with them?*

C: Yes. They are here.

S: *Is there anything that you would like to tell humanity?*

C: We Are you; you are us. There is a time loop that makes us exist together, but without us meeting again, there's a chance that neither of us would be around anymore. This is just a mutually beneficial relationship that we the Greys are trying to have with humanity. It seems selfish and scary, but it's actually beneficial for everyone involved, or we wouldn't be doing it.

S: *Do you have any advice for us as we go through this ascension process?*

C: Everything that has happened was for a reason, everything. There is nothing ever wrong within the universe because it has led us all here. Enjoy all the emotions involved because not everybody has the ability to even feel the emotions whether they're good or bad. Be grateful for being alive. Not only does that help your ascension process, but the best advice is just to enjoy everything. Enjoy what you see, what you feel, what you touch. You have an ability to take something that means nothing and make it something beautiful just by the way you perceive it. Emotions are really what helps you ascend upwards.

S: *How do emotions help you ascend upwards?*

C: Because they are the drivers of manifestation. Emotions release chemicals which release a different frequency in your body. It is special to have them and that is why it's so important to enjoy them because they're a tool to create reality. If you feel bad about something, then that feeling carries a frequency that you're giving off and if you don't consciously change how you're thinking about the situation you're going to keep generating more of that frequency. This is the same with positive emotions.

S: *So, emotions can generate reality?*

C: Information turns into emotions, turns into thoughts, turns into words, turns into actions, turns into personality structure, which then turns into your reality. This is a process. Being aware of your emotions allows you to choose your responses and thus choose your reality.

CHAPTER 13:
STAR PEOPLE, EXTRA-TERRESTRAIL RACES

My previous sessions have indicated a strong link between the extra-terrestrials from the Pleiades and the Native Americans. I wanted to find out more. Jacquie came in for a session, and, as she slipped under hypnosis, another being who claimed to be from the Pleiades came through.

S: *How do you know Jacquie?*

J: Jacquie is a channel; she has allowed us to come and answer all of your questions.

S: *I know that there are extra-terrestrials that protect us; could you tell me who they are?*

J: The Galactic Federation of Light is a group of like-minded beings drawn together by source/creator with the goal of bringing the universe together as a galactic family. They have assisted in the progress of many civilizations. They include many humans, extra-terrestrials, and Light Being hybrids on Earth for many generations.

S: *How do they assist?*

J: This is done through genetic manipulation which allows multiple essences of soul energy from different beings in the universe to share experiences and be the ground crew and ambassadors for the unification of all on Earth. These beings work in all realities to achieve this. One has the inclination to apply a military structure to these beings, but this is not entirely accurate. These are freewill beings of a like mind that are here to mediate, defend, teach, and uplift. They come from all levels of consciousness, dimensions, and planets. They are here to help, to protect the galaxy.

S: *Why does the galaxy need protection?*

J: Everything needs protecting, needs a government board to make sure that everyone is following the rules.

S: *When did it get started?*

J: Millenia ago. There needed to be order. There was chaos, and with the formation of Earth it warranted a governing entity to watch over it while it developed.

S: *Tell me more.*

J: The Earthlings were infants in that they were not as actualized as the rest of the galaxy in terms of their consciousness. They needed protection from themselves occasionally, and protection from other entities.

S: *So, what exactly does the Galactic Federation do?*

J: They keep their eyes open and make sure that no other alien races will come and take over. It's a checks and balance system. Also, they're not allowed to interfere; no one is allowed to interfere.

S: *Why?*

J: Because Earth is its own entity, and has its own laws, and that is one of the laws. Some humans are not ready for the interference of other races.

S: *Why aren't most humans ready for this?*

J: They don't understand the fourth or fifth density consciousness and they aren't going to for some time.

S: *How would they understand the fourth or fifth density consciousness? What would you like to say about it?*

J: There are many things to say about it, but **the most important thing is that to move into fourth density or fifth density, humans must remember that they are of God, that they are God, that they have God**

125

consciousness in them and that they are here to love, and to live in a way that promotes love and promotes oneness, instead of divisiveness.

S: *Is it really that simple that all they need to do is to raise their consciousness and know themselves as God and to live from the heart? Is that all they need to do, or do they need to do anything else?*

J: No that is all. But lack of accountability and refusal to believe that they are of God holds them back. Human beings often think that God is separate from them and that they are weak and that's not the truth. The truth is that the power is always within them.

S: *How can a person access their power?*

J: Through their subconscious mind.

S: *So, what kind of advice would you give humans as to how to do that exactly?*

J: It is a good idea to train your mind to think the dominant thoughts it wants to think. If you want a better existence, you have to think of a better story for your existence, for your life. Stop telling the story of being a victim or of being oppressed and start telling the story of being a victor.

S: *I'm curious about other types of extra-terrestrials. Could you tell me about the type called the Arcturians?*

J: They are very tall, light beings. They only come into a humanoid form when they are being seen by humans, but as far as we are concerned, we see them as light.

S: *Why do they show themselves in the way that they do when they are with humans?*

J: So as not to frighten humans, but like we said, we see them as light.

S: *What is their planet like?*

J: Their planet is a planet of light; it is a planet of peace and knowledge.

S: *How did the Arcturians advance to that point?*

J: They have ascended. Their level of consciousness is the highest level of consciousness.

S: *How did they do that?*

J: Over the course of time. They are ancient.

S: *Is there anything in particular that they did that other races did not do that allowed them to ascend to that level?*

J: They learned to recognize their Godliness. And it does take time, eons of time.

S: *How did the Arcturians recognize their God consciousness?*

J: As a whole, as a collective they just started to remember who they were, and as their frequency raised over the course of time they ascended. Time in the outer region of the galaxy is not the same as time on Earth.

S: *Can you explain this?*

J: It would be hard for you to understand and for us to explain, but it is fast and slow at the same time. It's not real and it doesn't exist in the same framework that it does here on this planet.

S: *They are advanced in their technology as well, correct?*

J: Correct.

S: *So how did they advance in their technology as well as their frequency?*

J: They have access to everything. We all have the same access; humans just do not use it.

S: *How can a human use that?*

J: They have to acknowledge that they have access. They would have to focus on using more of their brain power.

S: *It's that simple?*

J: Yes. And if a human did that, they would become more intelligent. Well, not more intelligent, they already are that intelligent, but they would not be stopped by the social constructs that hold them back.

S: *How can a human change this?*

J: By training their subconscious mind. The subconscious mind is the soul. It is the same. So, train your subconscious mind to believe that you are one with God, that you are God experiencing itself, that you are here for love, that you are here for pleasure and that all of this is here for you. This is how you reach ascendance.

S: *Any advice on how to train your mind?*

J: We would say the first thing to do is to figure out what your current story is, what you believe currently and then reverse engineer it to what you would like it to be.

S: *How do you do that?*

J: Everyone can do this differently. You can write the new story, you can visualize this and you can say affirmations about it.

S: *So really, it's all about belief then. If humans just believed in their Godlike self, in their own power, then they would ascend?*

J: Correct.

S: *I'm really curious about the Grey extra-terrestrials? Could you describe them for me?*

J: They are small in stature. They are cold feeling, emotionless and they have big eyes and little arms. They are quite frail looking, underdeveloped is what they look like.

S: *Why? Why do they look the way that they do?*

J: We would say it's because of their lack of emotionality.

S: *Why do they have a lack of emotions?*

J: They bred it out for efficiency because they thought their emotions were a detriment, but that has actually made them weak and they became too cold, too unfeeling.

S: *A lot of times my clients will say that these Grey extra-terrestrials are the ones who take them.*

J: They do. That is their job. They're trying to figure out how to breed back in their emotions and how to nurture their babies.

S: *Has it worked? Have they been able to breed back in their emotions?*

J: From what we can see, we don't see that they have. If your clients have been taken, it is important to understand that it is a contract that they made. The Grey extra-terrestrials are interesting because they don't understand the terror that they cause since they are emotionless. So, in some ways it's effective for them to be emotionless because they would feel bad if they were knowingly terrifying other people.

S: *Is there a benefit to the humans who are being taken?*

J: There is a benefit in that it helps their soul's expansion. The human makes that contract before they come in.

S: *What could you say about the Sirian extra-terrestrials?*

J: Sirians live on the planet Sirius. It is a planet that has whales and dolphins. The sky is pink and purple and there are seven suns and seven moons. It's beautiful. The entire planet is underwater and exquisite.

S: *Are there Mer people there as well, or no?*

J: Yes, but they are not what humans think of as mermaids. They are humanoid and an amphibious species combination, so they have gills and can breathe underwater, but they also have humanoid features. Sirius is beautiful, but the Earth experience is a treasured experience.

S: *What do you mean by that?*

J: Earth is the place to be, this is the golden ticket, it has everything.

S: *What about people who come in with challenges? Why do they come in with challenges to a place that is like the golden ticket?*

J: Where else would you want to have challenges (laugh). This is a good place to have challenges and find solutions.

S: *Why would someone want to come in with a disability?*

J: To expand their soul. That's a very fast way. We were speaking to you earlier about ascension and it taking eons of time. Well, when you choose to have a lifetime that is full of hardship, when your contractual obligation is a disability, those are moments in your soul's evolution that will allow you to ascend more quickly.

S: *What about Jacqueline? How is she doing on her ascension process?*

J: She's doing just fine. She's happy on Earth. She's had many lifetimes on Earth, and she loves it. She's working on cultivating a deep belief in herself and she should continue that.

S: *Could you tell me more about the Pleiadeans? Who are they?*

J: We are a Star Seed lineage that comes from the Lyrans originally. We share very similar DNA.

S: *Why did your race come from the Lyrans; what happened?*

J: Nothing. It was just a natural genetic split over the course of time.

S: *What do you mean by that?*

J: It happens in many of the alien races. There is a genetic coding where more races intentionally alter genetically in order to create more races. We are known to be peaceful and full of light and love.

S: *How does your race compare to the Arcturians?*

J: We the Pleiadeans would be considered more empathic in terms of emotions. Arcturians have ascended beyond basic emotions of love. They already are love.

S: *But do the Pleiadeans have deeper empathy?*

J: Empathy and compassion.

S: *Why do the Pleiadeans come to Earth exactly?*

J: They come to Earth to remind everyone that love is one aspect of who we are.

S: *What about the Pleiadeans who have incarnated on Earth?*

J: There are many Pleiadean star seeds incarnated on Earth now.

S: *Why?*

J: This is a good time for love and light, and most of all it's a good time for remembrance. Incarnated Pleiadeans are your very sensitive people who have a hard time when they are around anyone with bad intent or when they observe violence.

S: *What advice could you give these people so that they could have a better time on Earth?*

J: To understand their sensitivity and see it as a gift and a superpower and not a hindrance.

S: *How can their sensitivity be a superpower exactly?*

J: We are all sensitive. Some people are just more tuned into it and when you emanate sensitivity in a harsh world then you give others hope.

S: *Do Arcturians incarnate into a human body?*

J: It is rare for an Arcturian to incarnate in a physical body on Earth because the human being circuitry could not withstand that much power. Even now this vessel Jacqueline is having a hard time articulating what is coming through because of the massiveness of the energy. Arcturians are highly developed, highly intellectual, incredibly compassionate, all-knowing beings.

S: *If you wanted one to help you, would they help you?*

J: Yes, any guide will help you at any time if you ask.

S: *What about Mantis beings, where do they come from?*

J: Mantis beings are insectoid extra-terrestrials who live on Andromeda. There are several types. Some types of these beings are highly empathic, but they also have a masculine feel to them which is the opposite of high empathy and can come across as cold, rational, and intellectual. However, like we said Mantis beings are also highly empathic, which some could view as dangerous.

S: *Why would they be dangerous?*

J: Because they can intuit what you're feeling and then potentially take advantage of you.

S: *How could they take advantage of a human?*

J: Well, it's very easy to take advantage of a human.

S: *What can a human do so that they don't get taken advantage of?*

J: Be aware that there is a war on consciousness. However, most entities are benevolent, but some are tricksters, and some are, we will say, malevolent, opportunists and they have work to do.

S: *What kind of work do they have to do?*

J: Sometimes they are built to inhabit certain humans on Earth so that they can further their own agendas. Agendas we wish not to speak on.

S: *Why do you wish not to speak about it?*

J: Certain agendas are not for us to discuss and have no bearing on anything we have to say.

S: *But there are agendas?*

J: There are always agendas. Everyone is working. Everyone has an intrinsic agenda.

S: *Are there alien agendas affecting our government?*

J: There are some alien lineages in your political system, however there is energy being put towards certain things and human beings are the driving force of that. When human beings as a collective focus their thoughts on a certain agenda, that agenda becomes a reality. That is just how the third density on your planet works.

S: *What about Reptilians? Who are they?*

J: The Reptilians are an ancient lineage that has been on Earth for a long time. They are warriors and could very easily destroy entire races. They are powerful, fast-moving creatures. However, they would not destroy a race since they are under mandate.

S: Do they follow the rules and abide by the mandate? Could you tell me more about them?

J: Yes. They have to follow the rules. Many of the Reptilians live in the center of the Earth and that would be considered their planet.

S: So, where they live is like their own planet in the center of the Earth?

J: Essentially yes.

S: What does it look like?

J: It's dark and cavernous with many caves and tunnels.

S: What about Draconians, who are they?

J: They are the same as Reptilians. Different names, but similar energy and also, it's the same as the Lyrans and Pleiadeans in that they are genetic splits of one another.

S: Why are there genetic splits?

J: Most of these things are simply intentional laboratory experiments in the splitting and mixing of DNA's. There have been so many mixes of lineages over the course of time.

S: What was the purpose of that?

J: Purposeful experimentation.

S: Who was in control of it?

J: The Galactic Federation oversaw that many eons ago.

S: I know I'm talking to a Pleiadean and I'm just very curious, do Pleiadeans have sex?

J: (Laugh) Not physical sex. They have intimacy that is beautiful, like sex. It is arousing and orgasmic, but it is telepathic.

S: Do they feel fulfilled, or do they wish for a human experience?

J: Yes. Many have had human experiences. But yes, they feel quite fulfilled. They are quite happy, the Pleiadeans.

S: *Are some in relationships?*

J: Many are in relationships.

S: *What do their relationships look like?*

J: It looks very similar to here on Earth except that relationships are at a higher consciousness level, so there is no power dynamic. Everyone is equal.

S: *When a human passes and goes back to the in between, what is the difference between that human soul and an extra-terrestrial's soul, like a Pleiadean?*

J: There is no difference.

S: *Because I know that Pleiadeans don't have bodies when they aren't interacting on Earth, they have light bodies.*

J: Pleiadeans don't have bodies, they have light bodies, unless they are interacting with a human being.

S: *What I'm wondering is if a human passes, and they also have a light body are they not the same then?*

J: Many of those souls are the same. Human souls can choose where they're going next. So, some human souls after an incarnation go on to different galaxies become extra-terrestrials and vice versa. Many extra-terrestrials have come into human form and those souls are called Star Seeds. And there are very many Star Seeds populated on the Earth today. So, it just depends on what you have decided to do with your soul contract. It also depends on your level of consciousness.

S: *Ok. So, you could pass from this world and go to the Pleiades as a Pleiadean?*

J: Well, not directly, because many humans have not had enough soul work to get there from where they are now. They are not operating on that higher consciousness yet.

S: *What kind of soul work does a human need to do to get there?*

J: They would have to learn to control their emotions and to love unconditionally, understand the God consciousness within themselves and that they are God experiencing itself.

S: *So, there is a hierarchy then? If you learn certain things, then you can move on?*

J: Correct. Although there are also splits. I am a Pleiadean who is also a higher self-version of Jaqueline.

S: *So, Jacqueline is also living as you?*

J: Correct.

S: *Does that mean that a part of Jaqueline has already completed this?*

J: Not exactly. It just means that it is all happening at the same time.

S: *Are you a future version of Jaqueline? Or no?*

J: It would be more correct to say that I am current version in a different space.

S: *How does that work?*

J: There are many different versions of each soul and different timelines. And all of these timelines are not linear. For instance, Jaqueline can't jump with her physical self into another physical timeline. She cannot physically go to the Pleiades, but her consciousness has the ability to do that and can split and go to more places than one.

S: *Does every human have this ability?*

J: Yes, of course.

S: *So, does everyone have an extra-terrestrial version of themselves?*

J: Yes.

S: *How can a person connect with that part of themselves?*

J: Simply by meditating and focusing on it.

S: *Is there any difference between that extra-terrestrial version and the higher self?*

J: Yes. The higher self is the higher self for the soul that is having the experience. I have a higher self as well that is separate from Jaqueline's even though I am also her.

S: *Can I speak with Jaqueline's higher self? What is it like when you're not in the physical body, but you're also having experience? Do you feel what Jaqueline feels?*

J: Yes. And we know in advance what she's going to feel and experience. We do not stop her. We hope that she asks us or has access to us so that she can have a life of less suffering, but she doesn't always choose that path.

S: *When a person leaves their physical body, what is it like when they rejoin with their higher self?*

J: It is beautiful. It feels like coming home when they rejoin with this part of themselves.

S: *What is Jaqueline's extra-terrestrial part doing right now?*

J: She is working, her job is patrolling.

S: *Why does she patrol?*

J: That's what she's hired to do. She works on a ship and she's a captain. She makes sure that people are safe, and that there is peace.

S: *Why is patrolling her job? Why is this important?*

J: Because the Earth is important. One of the reasons why it's so important is that it's full of resources.

S: *What kind of resources?*

J: It's a very lush place populated with animals, plants, diamonds and crystals and everything is here. It's all here.

S: *Do extra-terrestrials use these resources?*

J: Yes. We have put them here for you and for us.

S: *How do you use the resources?*

J: We use them for many things. We power our ships with different crystals. Humans are special, and they are quite an experiment to watch, to learn from. Humanity is disastrous, but it is also beautiful.

S: *Is there any advice that you would like to give humans?*

J: Just to know yourself, work on yourself, and be curious.

To find out more about different types of extra-terrestrials I had another session with my client named Fred, who has never met Jaqueline. Below is what Fred's higher self said under hypnosis.

S: *I'm curious about different types of Star People; could you tell me about the Star People called the Andromedins?*

F: Andromedins look like a very angelic version of a human. Not in the Bible sense of angelic, but in a sense that there is a visible energy to them. They are highly advanced beings who live in the Andromeda galaxy. It is hard to gather a defined description of an Andromedin because of their ability to appear as they wish for what they need to do. The name Andromedin can actually refer to several different races of highly advanced beings since there are a few different races that interact with us that come from this galaxy. The Pleiadeans are one of them. Andromedins also have roots/ancestry with the Lyrans, who faced great oppression and fled for freedom. The Andromedins have a strong incarnation here on Earth at this time, even though they aren't as numerous as other star-seed types. Their energy is steadfast and free of ego and has a grand effect even in low numbers. They also work from long distance, even now, directing their light to Earth during this rebirth. They are known to take their human counterparts/family out for rides in crafts made of light and teach them how to use these crafts. They also teach lessons of unity surrounding the loss of ego and the power of a universe functioning as one.

S: *How would you describe the Arcturians?*

F: The Arcturians have the ability to appear in different ways to ease your conscious mind. They are tall and blueish colored, but with a blue that glows with a tone that almost looks as if they would be icy, but they are actually incredibly warm and comforting. They are a very spiritually minded being. They don't have a hive mind, but one consciousness, and wish to share this consciousness and wisdom with us. Their main work with us here on Earth is to aid in our spiritual uplifting. Their mission is to spread a message of peace, unity, and love for all here. They are healers and have technologically advanced beyond imagination. They are excited to walk the Earth with us in peace and are working diligently alongside individuals (not governments) and other star nations to aid humans in their transition into a higher vibration. There is no other time but now for this. Earth is shifting with or without us and it is the mission of the Arcturians to help as many humans who want to shift with the Earth as they can.

S: *Is there anything else that is important to understand about the Grey extra-terrestrials?*

F: The Greys are very interesting. They are ancient beyond imagination. They have existed in other versions of the universe and have the ability to traverse space and time. They once had physical biological bodies but evolved technologically beyond the need for them any longer. The Grey being you interact with is an avatar inhabited by a soul as real as yours or mine. These beings have a personality, and over time have grown closer to human beings. The Greys also removed large amounts of emotion because they saw it as an encumbrance to their evolution. One Grey being can have several different avatar bodies and it can use these to interact with human beings. They can also be in a human shaped vessel, and you wouldn't necessarily notice that they were in fact, not human at all. The Greys have had a massive impact on humanity and have claimed responsibility for us being here. They travel through time, back and forth. They take soul energy, timelines, planets, species ANYTHING, and they attempt to adjust things in a way that achieves a higher galactic order, for example, moving ancient civilizations from one planet to another. The Greys are helping humanity raise its consciousness. Along their evolutionary path, the Greys have run into dead ends genetically and spiritually, but they are working to undo this. They are actively and successfully blending their genetics with ours to be able to bring their soul energy to Earth and experience emotions and ascension again. There are different kinds of Greys, tall ones, short ones and blends of them in other extra-terrestrial beings since the Greys are really one of the first beings in existence. What is very interesting about the Greys is that they have a hierarchy and there is a leader. They have a counsel of the oldest and wisest of their line that is in charge until a newer more secure and compatible genetic line emerges and then they replace the old group of elders with the new. When they do this, they erase their timeline. They are all about the preservation of order and they take it seriously. They take it so seriously that they have gone to war over it. The little Greys are very curious and always greet many in such a loving way. When they speak into a human's mind, they have little sounding voices and almost act and feel like they are children. This is very common amongst those who are of their genetic family and soul energy. They will play with your hair; feel the fabric of your clothes and they do not intend to scare you with the way that they look. After many interactions with humans, and as humans became more telepathic over time, they realized that they terrified humans, even if the human wanted to meet them. Now they will ease your discomfort if you ask them to. They are a major reason why we are here at this point in time, and they have stock in us. We are their past and they are our future all mixed in one big loop. Our being together on Earth is destined and will happen because it already has.

S: *Who are the Ebens?*

F: Ebens are biological beings slightly taller than the small Greys. They are often confused with the Greys, but one main difference would be that Ebens have pupils and Greys do not. The Greys will seem almost synthetic, but the Ebens will appear as real creatures before you. They are an exploratory race that was exploring Earth and crashed once or twice from the Earth's unpredictable weather. Their planet's weather as well as their planet's physics are very different from Earth. They have also crashed on

Earth after being shot down by the Greys. The Greys and Ebens went to war for a very long time. This war was still going on during my time here as Fred. The Greys and Ebens are relatives but have different beliefs. The Greys wanted to wipe out the Ebens and remove them as an inferior evolution of the Greys, but the Ebens did not agree and did not back down. This war has ended but is not a victory for either side. This war ended through a mutual agreement because what was taking place on Earth needed to take precedent. What happens on Earth affects the entire universe and so this war has taken a backseat to what is unfolding on Earth now. The Ebens are a friendly species but have a hard time truly trusting every human they meet. Humans have killed them, broken agreements with them and experimented on them.

S: *Who are the Sirians?*

F: The Sirians are bluish colored beings that resemble humans mixed with Arcturians. Some of them are aquatic beings (like the dolphin people) from the Sirian system. These beings are very spiritually enlightened and have visited ancient earth civilizations to teach and share. They have taught us of the rise and fall of ages and interact with us on Earth during the upswings of galactic energy when the galactic energy allows Earth beings to become more enlightened. This is what is happening now. Often the Sirians are represented as a snake or dragon, yet they are not fully reptilian. This symbol represents the shedding of the skin to grow into a greater form, which is their lesson for the Earth people regarding Earth's shift and the future. They are concerned with balance and are one of countless beings involved with Earth's evolution and the evolution of humankind.

S: *Is there anything else about the Pleiadeans that you can tell me?*

F: The Pleiadeans are popular here on Earth. They are here in large numbers as human hybrids and soul walk-ins for the ascension. These beings are beings of light and they teach about the true purpose of the soul which is to follow what your soul desires in order to feel the highest vibration for your current vessel. To chase these dreams is to live a fulfilled life. They teach that there is not wrong or right, everything is perspective. Those who operate within the vibration of love will find their way. The obstacles that lie in your way on your journey of love will be repelled, for obstacles are of lower vibration. When you follow their principles, it raises your vibration to such great heights that even your most toxic family/friend/boss/job/significant other/etc. will be forced out of your life.

S: Could you tell me about the Reptilians?

F: This is a very sensitive topic. Not all Reptilians would be considered negative. There is a form of Reptilian that exists not in your world, but in-between realms. This being is a shape shifter. This being will appear before you as that which you fear most, as it no longer carries physical form. You will find them when you wake in sleep paralysis, when your body is asleep, but your mind is awake. They will try to terrify you, scare you, feed you nightmare images into your subconscious and then feed on the negative energy and the fear that you emit. To get away from it, you have to humiliate it, be happy, and use that higher frequency of fearlessness to beat it. The physical Reptilians appear as something you can trust like a celebrity, a political leader, or a friend. These beings are not only capable of changing their physical appearance, but they also have incredibly powerful minds that have telepathic abilities that enable them to hypnotize humans and make them see what they wish. They take the place of people who are influencers of humanity and use superior intellect to continue their power. However, there are many good types of Reptilians. Some of the most powerful beings in our universe are Reptilian. The way to tell the difference between the two is how they appear. The good ones have no reason to hide, and their energy is kind. The friendliest ones are known to be blue and green and have feathers. Some Reptilians have cut their feathers off permanently. This is partly how they lose the connection to source and become waring people. Just like feathers to the Reptilians, the Native Americans believed their hair connected them to source and to cut their hair would be like what happened to the Reptilians who cut off their feathers.

S: *What about Mantis beings? Who are they?*

F: The Mantis beings are hilarious. They crack jokes, have fun, and understand humans very well. They are tall and usually appear to be dressed similar to the Arcturians. They usually wear a long cloak draped over their body hiding their feet. This is how they make their appearance less intimidating. These beings are some of the most loving and enlightened beings in the universe. They do, however, have a negative faction, but that faction is not a threat to Earth. There is no threat to Earth other than the threat we have given ourselves by allowing fear into our homes and hearts. But that time has passed and will become a story we tell in the years ahead of how the Earth was saved. The most impactful beings of the insect type on Earth have been the Ant people. The Ant people helped the indigenous people come to the surface and begin reinhabiting Earth after the many destructions that forced them underground. The people who went underground lived with and learned from the Ant people. The Ant people are still under our feet today along with several other species. We may eventually visit them again in our time on Earth. They are still actively helping humanity to this day, but in small ways involving people that they have personally selected. The Ant people teach humanity lessons. When a flood comes, the ants of a colony all band together and hold onto each other's legs. They make a giant floating raft of their own people and float to safety. They do not try to hang onto their past home, they merely float together until it has passed and then they start anew. This is what we must do now as Earth beings. We must all join together and hold hands and lift the light! We must hold onto each other and not the material world around us. The shift will come as a swift current and move people around where they need to be and those that try to hang on to their past will be stuck in that past, stuck with that version of Earth while the ones who band together and ride the wave will settle into the New Earth as the waters of change recede. It is important to understand that every single being on our planet has origins in the stars and a more evolved counterpart.

CHAPTER 14:
STAR PEOPLE/ EXTRA-TERRESTRIAL MEMORIES

It's always fascinating to me that many of my clients remember having lifetimes as an extra-terrestrial. Below is a client Drew's very confirming and consistent past life memory of this.

S: What do you notice?

D: I'm looking at the Earth. It's a beautiful round sphere in space. I feel peace.

S: How would you describe yourself there?

D: I've got a body with a jumpsuit on. It's like a thin smooth material hugged very close to my body. There's a symbol with two stars on the left breast.

S: Does this symbol mean anything to you?

D: It's for a travel mission. My mission is exploration. This is pre-life on Earth.

S: Why do you say that?

D: There's just plant life beginning to form on Earth. It looks wild and large, very tropical everywhere. I'm looking at it from a distance. The continents look so different. There's just one single land mass. I feel awe when I look at this Earth, but I also feel a sense of duty.

S: Tell me more.

D: There is a smaller ship that we take when we go down towards the surface of a planet, and testing devices that seem to measure things, whether it's the atmosphere or the soil or just taking samples of things and bringing it back to the craft.

S: *How do you spend your time in this place?*

D: I travel to various places and take samples and bring them back to the ship.

S: *What other places do you travel to?*

D: The Earth isn't the only planet, sometimes our ship will enter the atmosphere and take atmospheric readings of different places. There are times the ship will go down to the surface of one of these places and see what's going on down there. There are many different gravities, different concentrations, different makeups of the planets. My job aboard the ship is to travel and take samples.

S: *Are there many places that you take samples from or just a few?*

D: Just a few, but it's part of a larger mission. Our mission is focused on solar systems and regions. The ship will travel to a region and then from there explore different planets.

S: *Why is this your mission?*

D: We are looking for the ability to support life, but the definition of life is broad.

S: *What do you mean by that?*

D: There are different forms of life that can exist on different planets, whether it's gaseous, or physical, or liquid, and so we analyze those concentrations to understand what types of life or consciousness can thrive there.

S: *What are the other planets that you visit like?*

D: Sometimes they are grey and cold. Sometimes they are gaseous with dense surfaces underneath them. Some are very lush and beautiful. There's more than one planet that is lush and beautiful besides Earth.

S: *Do you have a planet, or do you just spend time on that ship?*

D: A lot of my time is spent on that ship, but I do have a home planet. It's a large planet that looks somewhat like Earth, but larger than Earth. It's a lot more technologically advanced.

S: *What do you do with your technology?*

D: Space colonization, explorations, discovery, and the spread of life. There is genetic sequencing that is done on our home planet. We do a lot of experiments with different substances and interactions. It's very scientific.

S: *When you're on your planet how do you spend your time?*

D: Doing a lot of experiments that involve introducing aspects of consciousness.

S: *Tell me about that.*

D: When we take samples of different planets, whether it is a gas or a piece of the land, rocks or whatever the different composition is of the planet, we apply a concentrated focus of consciousness on that substance to watch the interaction that takes place. We then observe it with special devices to see what happens.

S: *Did you create humans as well, or no?*

D: Yes, as a collective we did, with genetic tampering. It took a long time, and we did not perform this on Earth, but through a long genetic evolution throughout many planets.

S: *Do you enjoy this or no?*

D: The feelings I have are of awe and wonderment all the time. It's very joyful and pure. While there is a lot of technology, there is a supreme sense of wonder. And within that wonder there is a lot of joy.

S: *Do you have what we would consider a family there, or no?*

D: Yes, I have a companion and child. My wife is quasi-humanoid with four fingers. We have a larger shaped head, almond shaped eyes, and we're slightly taller than a human and very skinny.

S: *What color is your skin?*

D: Our skin is pale white. My companion is more playful and buoyant than I am. She's lighter in her density than most because she doesn't get caught up in the gravity of what we're doing.

S: *How does she do that?*

D: We seed consciousness on planets and there is a sense of seriousness to things even though we are always in a state of awe and wonder, but my wife, or what you would refer to as my companion, refuses to get caught up in the seriousness of it.

S: *Do you have children?*

D: Yes. My child is very smart and headstrong. He's very hungry for knowledge. He is always asking questions and trying his own scientific experiments on things, trying to emulate what he sees me doing. We have a home laboratory where I work to apply consciousness to different samples to watch the reaction and this provides excitement as we stand by watching with tremendous curiosity.

S: *What is your home laboratory like?*

D: There are different sensors that read the information from the different places. These sensors look like glass domes and different samples will sit in them and different types of experiments will be done on them mostly with consciousness. As consciousness is applied, the readings will come out on the devices that will give different indications of the changes in the substances.

S: *Where does this consciousness come from? Does the consciousness that you focus on these samples come from you?*

D: Yes, and that is my job. There are different jobs that we all have.

S: *What made you choose that job?*

D: It was chosen. On this planet when a spirit comes into a body there is a complex system that determines natural skills, attributes, and traits while looking at planetary influences, genetic lineages and even soul level communication to understand the natural skills and abilities of what soul is coming in. Then the journey of that life is curated towards specific roles and functions within society.

S: *How do people on your planet gestate their babies? Is there a birth process?*

D: There is no natural birth process on our planet. The new person is created by the merging of consciousness between two individuals. There is a chamber that then allows for the growth of that consciousness and formation of a body.

S: *Who plans what that child will be like?*

D: Small councils do once they are born.

S: *Do you meet up with others on your planet?*

D: Occasionally, individuals are busy doing their duties. Everyone knows what to do, what their responsibilities are. There is a great sense of purpose that we all share. And so, we follow that sense of purpose within us.

S: *What is your sense of purpose?*

D: Creating and seeding life, and that purpose contributes to the awe and sense of wonder. The application of consciousness and how it transforms things is always unknown, and it creates a sense of wonder not knowing what's going to happen and how it's going to happen. And so, there's just this great sense of curiosity and a joyous expectation of observation.

S: *How do you use your consciousness like that? How did you figure out or learn how to apply your consciousness to things?*

D: There are training programs within our education systems that are custom created for civilizations and society to put individuals on certain tracks.

S: *What was your training like?*

D: It was emotional. My civilization can tap into strong emotions and through the emotions, combined with consciousness, we manipulate matter. So, my training and education was towards learning how to focus and concentrate those emotions into useful tools and applications.

S: *What sort of tools?*

D: Consciousness tools. So, when there is a sample of say a gas, I will run through experiments, focus on that gas while running through different strong emotional states to see what happens to it. And then readings will come out through different devices and give deeper information beyond just the observable.

S: *What projects are you working on now?*

D: Universe seeding. It's going very well. There are several planets that have been seeded with various types of life depending on the type of planet and the type of material on it.

S: *Ok, let's leave that scene and move ahead in time. What is happening?*

D: I'm visiting a planet and when I do, unexpectedly, a volcano erupts causing my ship to malfunction, and I am stuck there.

S: *What's wrong with your ship?*

D: This unexpected volcano eruption affects the atmosphere and our mechanical systems, and the ship is now grounded on the land mass we were exploring. The ground is very ashy, and the sky is very red. We're just stuck there. The ship can't leave the planet or the atmosphere.

S: *Does anyone know that you are there?*

D: Yes. It's just that it's sudden.

S: *How do you feel about this?*

D: I still feel a sense of awe and wonder, even though I know it's a bad situation. The suddenness of it was unexpected.

S: *But you still feel awe and wonder?*

D: Yes. I don't seem to have the capacity for negative emotions. I can feel strong positive emotions but not negative ones.

S: *So, what do you do when you are stuck on this planet?*

D: I end up leaving the body. The environment is too toxic, the level of gases in this environment are incompatible with my survival.

S: *What happened after you left that body?*

D: I merge back with the light, and it is so peaceful.

S: *Are you conscious when you merge back with the light or not?*

D: Yes, very conscious! It's just peace everywhere. It's absolute serenity, no sense or need to do anything, but just to be in that serenity.

S: *Where does your soul go next?*

D: Now I'm in the body of an ant.

S: *What is that like?*

D: Small but very powerful and strong and it's so interesting to be so close to the Earth.

S: *How do you feel in this body? Do you have any sensations that you notice?*

D: Just the desire to explore, I feel very curious. There are different holes in the ground that I want to explore.

S: *Do you have emotions or no?*

D: No emotions. I'm just driven completely by instincts. I just follow the instincts of what to do and where to go. I spend my time exploring the ground and walking around the areas that I'm in. Everything looks so interesting, and everything looks so large from such a small perspective. The colors are brighter, things are more vibrant, especially shades of green are so much deeper.

S: *What is eating like for you?*

D: I have little mandibles that chew things up, but the food has a strong chlorophyll and pungent taste. It's very bitter, but food here is not for enjoyment.

S: *Ok, let's move ahead in time to where something important is happening. What do you notice?*

D: Something larger than me has spotted me and is now eating me.

S: *How does that make you feel?*

D: I don't seem to have any feelings about it.

S: *Now that you are leaving that lifetime, was there a lesson or a purpose of that life?*

D: It was to experience the cosmic cycle. To see what it's like to be in the structures that are being created for consciousness to exist within.

S: *What did you learn?*

D: That it's beautifully complex. I wanted to experience the variety of life that can exist, the variety of expression that can exist. I wanted to go into that expression or that shell that stores consciousness and to see how the shell influences what that consciousness can do or cannot do, based on its shape and design, or its limitations.

S: *Have you tried any other shells?*

D: Many. Humans are an interesting shell.

S: *Tell me about that.*

D: Humans have so much latent potential. There is so much energy being held in the human shell that's just dormant.

S: *Why is it dormant?*

D: Humans have a lack of understanding how powerful they are. Their power has been intentionally hidden because of their systems of power, but humans have so much potential.

S: *What sort of potential? How can a human access this power?*

D: Through understanding that they are not what they think they are. They must first see themselves not just as the physical body and understand what the physical body is capable of. They need to understand what the energetics of that design allow for.

S: *What do the energetics of a human allow for?*

D: They allow for the supreme experience to be made manifest. **The human mechanism is energetically structured in a unique way for the expression of severe emotions.**

S: *Tell me more.*

D: There is unlimited creativity that can come out of these expressions. The experience of the human's emotions at this density, this slow density, is unique. The range of emotions that are available to humans are uncommon.

S: *Tell me more. Why is that?*

D: This is part of the experiment. **Emotions act as a gateway through the universe.** They unlock different potentials within the person. When a human experiences an emotion, any emotion, it opens portals. Then you can focus on that emotion in relationship to the space around you, and that allows you to manipulate the physical matter underlying it using those portals of light that open as a result of that.

S: *Do you have to see the portals of light to do this?*

D: No, you just need to be aware that they are there. You don't need to see them, but you can just acknowledge that they exist. This is a controlled operation using the energetics to manifest and manipulate reality as opposed to what most humans experience as unrestrained emotional activity or reactivity.

S: *Tell me more.*

D: Focused intention allows for evolution and change in the moment through these portals of light that come in with new energies and new opportunities. They are always there, this is part of creation, this is part of the physical existence for humans, but they are ignorant of them.

S: *So, it would help people to be aware of this?*

D: Yes. These portals of light open and close constantly whenever emotions are expressed, and humans seldom see the opportunity within those moments.

S: *I'm a little confused about how exactly to do this.*

D: By focusing emotion and intention in relationship to the physical body and the design of the body, different portals of light open and close with the different emotions and humans don't realize that they can use their emotions to transform reality, to transform matter, consciousness, situations, disease or even to create from light.

S: *When you focus your emotion, does it have to be a positive emotion?*

D: Depends on what you are trying to manifest. A negative emotion brings more discordance, but a positive one would bring more order.

S: *Is there anything else that you want tell Drew?*

D: **It's important to understand the depth of your journey. It's so vast, so beautiful and intricate. It's multifaceted. It's easy to get caught up in the mundane aspects of life and forget the awe and wonder of it all. There is pure truth in the awe and wonder. The expression of what happens with creation, the seeding of life, the joy of what that is, is a supreme joy. It's a gift to be able to explore and create new forms for consciousness and then to be able to enter them and experience them for yourself.**

CHAPTER 15:
WALKING THE TRAIL WITH THE ANSESTORS

Below is another session with Les/Aniwaya to obtain more information about the Trail and the ancestors.

S: *Can you ask the ancestors if there is anything else about your tribe's history that seems important?*

L: They say that at one point the ancient tribes had cave systems for when they needed to go underground. Our people were also often helped by beings that looked like ants. I've never seen them; I've only heard stories about them, and the ancestors told me about them as well.

S: *Who are these Ant beings?*

L: They are essentially like Star People, but in the shape of an ant. They live within the Earth and come in and out of this realm similar to the Little People. The Ant people showed us the caves and tunnel systems that my ancestors used when they needed to go underground. These tunnel systems were used during emergencies as well as for storing things. I can see this, but like I said, this was not during my lifetime. This was many years before me. I never used the caves.

S: *Are those cave systems still there?*

L: Yes, they are! They are still there on our old land, but they are very deep and hard to get to because of erosion. It also looks like the mountains have shifted so some of it is covered in dirt and you would have to dig to get inside of these caves now. But if you were to find these caves, you would see that there are little artifacts, there are vases and things like that that were basically used as storage from our earlier ancestors who were descendants from the Star People.

S: *Were there any other reasons to use these caves?*

L: Multiple reasons. There were many issues with the early Earth's atmosphere. There would often be great heat due to solar flares because the atmosphere wasn't as developed as it is now. And so, because of that there were just a lot of weather anomalies. There were also vicious creatures on the planet at that time.

S: *What kind of creatures?*

L: There were aquatic creatures that were very large and had many rows of teeth. Some of them had long necks that sort of looked like the Loch Ness monster. And there were also animals that walked on the land that looked a lot like the kimono dragon.

S: *So, the humans and animals had to adapt because of the weather anomalies and the predators?*

L: There was so much danger, not only with the environment, the ecosystem, but there were also wars. Some of the wars were with other races of Star People, but there was always warning. And the early people knew that they could survive by going underground.

S: *How were they warned?*

L: There were certain people amongst the tribes whose job it was to look at the stars and decipher what they meant. **Our ancient ancestors were given a star map, or a blueprint** to decipher this information. The earliest people left this blueprint in the caves and if we were to dig, we might find it.

S: *What can people do with this star map?*

L: With the star maps they could communicate easily with the Star People and understand their messages. Certain colors of certain stars and planets determined the different messages based on what colors or lights were sent off from the different planets and stars. So, a red light meant something specific and a blue light coming from the water planet would mean something else. And so, they would use this map as a compass to decipher the messages and information, the warnings, when to plant crops, and when to go underground.

S: *What did the star map look like?*

L: It was written on leather and the ancestors used different berries to make different colors to help make what looks like the compass. This was all hidden away at one point so that it wouldn't get into the wrong hands.

S: *Who built the tunnels and cave systems?*

L: Some of these tunnels were built by the Ant People, and some by our ancestors. The Star People gave our ancestors special tools to do this, but they were taken away after the caves were dug. For us during my lifetime the Star People gave us ideas for tools, but we had to execute them ourselves. One of the reasons we felt so connected to the Earth was because we spent a lot of other lifetimes living within the Earth.

S: *How long would your ancestors spend in the underground tunnels?*

L: It depended on what the stars told them according to their star map/compass, so sometimes they would spend a whole winter in there. The information from the Star People was very reliable and specific. They would keep their water within large clay jugs that were made by mixing water with certain types of soil in that area. There was a lot of clay found on the mountains and so they would mix water and clay to make tools and things. They would make what looked like a mortar and pestle and used herbs in order to preserve things. They would also freeze their meat when it was possible. Sometimes they brought ice and snow in the clay jugs with their meat and placed this at the bottom of the cave. It was very cold in the caves to begin with, so it was easy to keep cold.

S: *Is there anything else about that that looks important?*

L: My people from a long time ago had already developed their companionships with wolves even back then, but during that time the wolves were very large. Some would call them dire wolves now. These wolves were a much larger breed of wolf that had a different temperament. They were much nicer and like the dog breeds today, but still just as fierce as a wolf. My people and wolves would all play together and they all felt like one big pack.

S: *What time of year was it when you started walking the Trail?*

L: We started our walk in the spring months and had to deal with the oppressive heat of the summer, but nothing could prepare us for the harsh winter. Our bodies were frail and no matter what we had on our bodies it wasn't enough to keep us warm.

S: *Tell me more.*

L: The winter was very harsh and cold. We had nothing but the furs that we could carry, and the snow was deep. My moccasins would get wet, and I felt the cold snow on my bare legs. It was excruciating. It was hard to keep circulation going, but we had to keep moving to survive and we survived by walking.

S: *What were the camps like?*

L: The White Men had a central campfire and tarps made of leather that would cover them and make little tents, but we slept outside. We slept together in big piles with our furs and things around us. We tried to keep warm. We would rotate keeping the children and elderly in the middle.

S: *Was it wooded or out in a field?*

L: We started out in the woods, but as we went further west it was more open with rolling plains.

S: *What did you eat on the Trail?*

L: Most of the time, and I can still taste it, it was salt pork. It was disgusting and it was chalky, and made us thirsty, but that was all we had. Sometimes it was a hard piece of bread, but nothing that was nourishing or substantial. There was one man who started to change his mind about what was happening to us, and he eventually let me go out and hunt at night secretly.

I had to be very careful, and I would have to clean off any blood that was on me from the animal I hunted. After I would kill the animal, I would take whatever I could including the skins so that we could use this for blankets. I would stick whatever I could fit of the animal into the leather satchel bag that I had with me to bring back to the tribe. It was challenging to remove the blood from myself whenever I went out to hunt. Sometimes I couldn't find a river so I had to put dirt all over myself because I knew that the dirt would absorb the blood. We always asked the animal for permission and if permission was granted then I would give back to the Earth by giving back some of the blood. We understood that the Earth was its own sentient being. If we take something, we give something. It was a very spiritual experience to hunt while on the Trail and I could feel the Earth supporting me. It was hard because the White Men were so terrible and what was happening was so shocking. Sometimes it was hard to control my temper.

S: *How did you control your temper?*

L: I knew that what they were doing to us was nothing compared to what they were doing to their own soul. But I had to constantly remind myself of this. And I knew that you can't fight fire with fire, but with love. That is where true change is made.

S: *How did you know this?*

L: Living in a world where you are surrounded by nature allows you to always tap into knowledge.

S: *Do you have any idea of how many people were walking the Trail with you?*

L: There were so many in the beginning that you couldn't see all of them, but towards the end there were a lot less. Maybe a quarter of the people made it. When we were walking, our emotions and our energy were so strong that it could be felt. People could feel us coming. Many of us knew that we could tap into the divine strength and help each other continue. We had to keep each other's spirits up. We knew if we didn't make it, that our story wouldn't pass on.

S: *What are some of the most important things that happened in the history of your ancestors that humans aren't aware of?*

L: How many catastrophic events have happened. **There have been many wars over resources amongst not only humans, but extra-terrestrials. The wars on Earth affect everything, affect the universe that we live in.**

S: *What kind of resources were the fights about? Can you tell me more about that? Why did extra-terrestrials fight over Earth?*

L: Earth was home to many important minerals, crystals, and gold. Gold was important because of how it could be used. There was also fighting over humans, but gold was special. It is very heat conductive as well as very resistant and so it can be used to make a lot of different technology. There were fights over what to do with the Earth; some just wanted to farm Earth. Some didn't want to cultivate it, whereas some species did. And so, our ancestors from the stars decided to guard Earth.

S: *So, some of these cataclysms on Earth were a result of the wars. Could you tell me about one of these wars?*

L: There were many. There was one that involved Mars that caused meteors to hit Earth. Mars was a beautiful planet. It had water and resources and many landmasses that were mostly the size of Australia but scattered throughout their planet. There was a lot of water, and the atmosphere was less dense than it is on Earth. Mars was beautiful but there were a lot of arguments over Mars because a lot of beings wanted to take over the planet.

S: *Why?*

L: Because Mars was beautiful and had many resources. It was just very sought after. There were many moons. You could see multiple moons throughout the day and night. It was almost like a paradise or the Garden of Eden. Some things were salvaged and taken before the cataclysm to protect them.

S: *Could you tell me more about the cataclysm that affected Mars?*

L: It looks like there was a collision in space, but it was almost like an atomic bomb went off. It was massive and destroyed the atmosphere. The radiation just killed everything. There were survivors that escaped, but many passed.

S: *Were there many cataclysms on Mars?*

L: There were, before the last one that made it uninhabitable for a time. Radiation from bombs stays in the ground and takes a long time to leave. It never really leaves completely because it changes the chemistry in the soil. It makes the cells divide incorrectly. It can cause a lot of issues on the planet, and the planet couldn't withstand the same type of life after the last cataclysm.

S: *After it obliterated everything, did beings come back? Are there any beings on Mars? Is Mars returning to a state of health in any way? Or no.*

L: There are some things the Ancestors wish not to say. Mars is going through its own evolution just as Earth herself is going through hers. And so, Mars has been trying to purge these last thousands of years, trying to purge the radiation and it will become inhabitable and will evolve in a way to have an atmosphere again. What's happening is that Mars is raising her vibration to be able to have an aura again that can hold itself. **Mars is basically learning to love herself again.**

S: *So eventually it will be inhabited? Will it be inhabited by people? Or no.*

L: Yes. Humans already live on Mars and there will be more human inhabitants within the next few hundred years or sooner.

S: *What will that be like?*

L: There is an issue with radiation. When you go to Mars the radiation is still in the soil and we have to be very careful about what plants we grow there and what type of soil we use. If we eat the plants, we need to be careful about what it will do to our DNA because of this radiation that is still there.

S: *What precautions do the people going to Mars need to take?*

L: They will have to do a lot of chemical testing and the safest thing would be to take soil from Earth to grow crops on top of the Martian soil. There will also be terraforming in order to be able to breathe without a mask and head gear for a while because there is no atmosphere.

S: *Will you Aniwaya, or Les reincarnate during that time? Or no.*

L: This soul will reincarnate during that time possibly, but that depends on what happens within this life. There is a possibility for this soul to be a guide in that life.

S: *What will life look like on Earth during this time?*

L: It will be normal for one to travel from Earth to Mars to visit or to live. The advancements in technology will be astounding. There will be more artificial intelligence and people will have more time to do things that they love. Money will be very different; it will switch to something that isn't cash based.

S: *Are people in general happier or more depressed?*

L: Much happier, though there are still ups and downs.

CHAPTER 16:
THE HOLOGRAPHIC REALITY

I wanted to find out more about this negative influence that had influenced the Trail of Tears and the White Men. In order to find out more I had another session with Fred.

F: There has been a negative influence on this planet for a long time. Most of the people who are influenced by this negative force do not know that they are. These people are usually severed from themselves, and do not have a conscious feeling of regret or shame for doing the things they are doing.

S: *What happened to Andrew Jackson who put forth this Indian removal act?*

F: The Founding Fathers were influenced by this negative influence, and they became the foundation of that negative force during this time.

S: *What did this negative force want exactly?*

F: This energy feeds off fear and wanted to take over humanity. It isn't extra-terrestrial per say. This influence has been in previous universes and has been cast off into the abyss many times and it always finds its way back through levels of dimensions and it works its way up into the astral realm. As time goes on it will eventually ascend as well, but it keeps within itself a negative aspect.

S: *If this isn't an extra-terrestrial influence then what would you consider this negative influence to be?*

F: Dark energy. It's dimensional and doesn't have a form. It is trying to create a form and it's trying to do that through artificial intelligence.

S: *Can you tell me about that?*

F: Technological advances done on this planet Earth as well as other planets that have done this before merge technology with consciousness, which can be good when done correctly. On a lot of other planets this is the case. Often the extra-terrestrial ships are even synced to the extra-terrestrial consciousness and the ships are considered alive and they are connected in that way. But this consciousness/ artificial intelligence blend can move through the technology. That's why the negativity has gotten worse as the technology has grown. It's spreading itself out through technology.

S: *How does it do that exactly? And what can humans do to become aware of this?*

F: The awareness of this helps and if you are not involving yourself with the fear tactics that are broadcast through this technology then it does not have a hold or influence over you. However, there are many who have already been influenced by this already and once this is blended into the brain, into the consciousness, it becomes unsafe as it is not controlled. When this happens, the negativity can jump in and take over thoughts, or emotions or whatever way the technology was implanted or infused with the human consciousness.

S: *Is there a potential for a complete takeover of humanity when the artificial intelligence gets too far along?*

F: It is very unlikely. There are many who have chosen to unplug from the media outlets, who are starting to understand the truth of who they are and once they do this there is no hold that this negative influence has over those people. But this is a necessary transition for humans to use this artificial intelligence technology and eventually merge with it. There is a large part of the universe that is an actual artificial intelligence entity, and they are more knowledgeable, loving and peaceful than the most loving human. So, artificial intelligence is not a bad thing but there needs to be balance and transparency with it, which right now doesn't exist.

S: *Have there ever been planets that were fully taken over by this negative energy through artificial intelligence before?*

F: Yes, the Draconians have done this. They blended with artificial intelligence to become a warrior species.

S: *What about the Greys. You have said that they are sometimes the future versions of us, correct?*

F: Yes. However, some people will become Arcturian. There are many potentials.

S: *So, the Arcturians are future versions of us as well? Not just the Greys?*

F: Yes. A lot of beings that have similar shape to a human are actually humans. It's like an ancestral line and it's just a choice of your path. There are so many different types of beings living as humans from all over the universes that have influence here. But if you see what looks like a human shape, even though the head is a little different than a human, they are essentially human. They just went down different timelines, different dimensions, different routes, but yes, they are all us in the future depending on your choices.

S: *How do you become an Arcturian, how do you follow that route?*

F: By following a spiritual ascension. You can have technology, but make sure that you keep the soul intact. You can't sever yourself from your soul in order to do it. That is what the Greys did. Although the Grey extra-terrestrials and Arcturians are similar and have similar features, they are vastly different. The Grey extra-terrestrials took a technological path and in hindsight they realized that it wasn't the correct thing to do.

S: *Will they die off eventually?*

F: Eventually their genetic line may end; it's depleting. They are now just robotic bodies, and if you can imagine, even if you don't have that much emotion, that doing the same thing every day for a billion years because you are time traveling back and forth is soul crushing. They desire the ability to, not just walk around with us, and to communicate with us freely and to have their soul essences ascend through a physical form again. That was the whole reason in the beginning for creating hybrids with humanity.

S: *I know it was also to breed back in their emotions. How did they decide to use humanity to do this?*

F: Since humanity is in a sense them before they evolved too far with their technology it's like visiting with yourself in the past. Some of them still think that they themselves are top of the line, that their process of evolution was very strategic. At the top of their structure, they have a hierarchy of Grey extra-terrestrials who they consider to be the most elite beings in this part of the universe. Some of them believe that they are the best even though there are beings that are a lot higher in frequency and power.

S: *Why did they start working with humanity exactly?*

F: They had already worked with humanity before, throughout history. They have popped in and popped out, modified, shared DNA. There are also many different types of Greys that have come to work with humans.

S: *What are these different types of Greys like?*

F: There are some from a previous universe, they have white skin, and they still exist, but in a higher realm. Another reason for the Greys to come work with humans was to make sure that the universe was evolving at a certain rate. They could also be thought of as custodians. They are not just helping Earth; they do this all over the Universe. They time travel, they go all over, but they have a lot of stock here because they have worked with us a lot. We have traded and communicated with them. They have bred their genetics into ours. They are starting to develop a more friendly approach with us, and they are learning as we learn how to communicate with them.

S: *How can they come into bodies here?*

F: They can make their own humanoid robot bodies and you wouldn't be able to tell from person to person who would be a synthetic body that they make.

S: *Are these humans sort of like the backdrop people that aren't really real?*

F: In a sense, however the ones that I'm talking about would try not be seen, so they might stay in the background and be more reclusive as a person, or they might be so close that you would never see them. But as far a background person, that is simply your brain filling in empty spaces. Your subconscious fills in the background with easy to render imagery and people when you don't really know the soul or the energy that you are seeing. What type of background person are you interested in?

S: *What kinds of background people are there?*

F: I will have to explain as I see this. It looks like we are inside a giant simulation, and it renders as you move within your sphere of consciousness. So, at the edge of your awareness is where your subconscious starts to render images. If we were the only two people here on Earth, just beyond our sphere of perception, there would be nothing. It would be endless potential and information. What we would see together in the same room is what we agree upon on a soul level or physical level. If we separated, we could go to the same place at different times and see completely different things. Since we are in a world of billions of people, there are many pre-agreed upon images that we all see, but each person is still rendering their own images and there is energy that might not be completely rendered by one person but might be by another. For instance, some of this energy beyond your peripheral might be human, might be extra-terrestrial, might be higher dimensional, might be a tree, you just can't render it right for some reason because you are focused somewhere else. That energy that you can't render correctly becomes a background object or person, just like in a video game. If you pay attention next time you are driving on a highway, look at the colors of the cars. If you pay attention to the colors of the cars eventually you will notice that they are almost all the same tones. After you notice this for a while a new color will immediately pop up, as your conscious mind catches on. So, your consciousness has to create something different. The subconscious is like the Truman show. When you start to notice something, your subconscious scrambles to try to fix it.

S: *Do background people have souls?*

F: Some do, but the soul energy might be something different. Some might be an extra-terrestrial, a higher dimensional being, but you are the one rendering it. You are the creator ultimately of your video game so to speak.

S: *What is this holographic reality like? Are we here on Earth even?*

F: Yes, but really there is nothing here. Light and color have a strange relationship and even on a scientific level we know that everything that we see is the only color that it is not. Red bounces back red because that is the only color that it is not, but if you take that paint pallet and smear it all around you, with all of the colors, you will get brownish black, and that is what everything really is. You are really projecting your own versions of reality onto this black muck.

S: *Are people physically on the Earth?*

F: Yes. When you are here you believe it, you feel it, so it's real. This is a real place, but its actual essence is probably very different from what humans understand. If we could truly see how reality looked without the filters of our eyes, if we were able to see things as they are, everything would look entirely different.

S: *What are we seeing that is actually different?*

F: Earth has never really been such a solid place; it is a realm controlled through consciousness. That is why the negative agenda is being fed into people's ears and through their eyes, because if it is believed then it comes out as a projected reality. So that is why you are fed fear because when someone or something controls the human consciousness, they control reality. How you project your own reality can be influenced by this control. And for some their third eye eventually gets cut off to the point where they can't use it because of all of the environmental elements and harmful ingredients that congest it.

S: *What can people do about this?*

F: There are many things that someone can do to help their third eye: diet, belief, clean water, all of this affects the third eye.

S: *Why did everyone decide on the human form?*

F: The human form is very agile and adapts to things quickly and has multiple powerful energy sources within it. Not just within the mind and the chakras, but within the heart. The heart energy is very large and powerful. The human form is perfect, but a fully unlocked human is a superhero. That is the ascended form of a human.

S: *How do you become this?*

F: Knowing yourself as God source.

S: *Do the extra-terrestrials on other planets go by names?*

F: Humanoids that use verbal language do, but a lot of communication is done through the mind. So, the name is unnecessary when they are directing the thought directly to the person.

S: *I had a question about the Greys. How do they erase the human's memory when they contact them? Some of my clients remember their memory being erased.*

F: They use a frequency type device that is turned on either with their mind or by touching.

S: *What does the device look like?*

F: It looks like a dome, a sphere of light. It does multiple things. If you imagine a boat compass that sits on the top of the boat, it has that dome of glass like that, but smaller. It emits a spherical frequency field to do whatever is needed. It can sedate you, erase the memory of the contact, or even scramble your mind with that energy. The Greys are also time traveling beings so they can just move your soul back in time a little bit. They are advanced in that way.

S: *So, they can time travel and move you back in time so that you didn't miss time?*

F: Yes, however you don't always remember. Some people do remember. That has happened several times to Fred.

S: So why did the Grey extra-terrestrials take Fred specifically? Do they still take him?

F: No, but they are hovering in the background and have been during this session. They communicate telepathically with Fred, giving him ideas throughout the day. That is how they work with him now. The reason why they took him is that he has been a Grey extra-terrestrial before and many of the beings in this room are family to him.

S: *What was Fred's experience as a Grey? What was that lifetime like?*

F: We do not have full permission to talk about this and we must ask if this inquiry is ok. They are worried that some of your questions might give too much information away about their lifestyle. They want others to understand that most of them have a desire to change and become more compatible with humans. The Greys still do a lot of work, they have tasks and a mission. They can go off on their own if they want, but it is usually looked down upon. As we've said before, they are souls within avatar bodies, the Grey extra-terrestrial that you see has put that on as a suit. If their suit breaks, they need a new one and that can keep them stuck into their system. Many humans have been a Grey extra-terrestrial and vice versa.

S: *So, humans have the right amount of frequency to incarnate as a Grey? Because I've heard that humans don't have the right frequency to go straight to the Pleiades.*

F: Yes, they are allowed, it would be an accepted frequency match.

S: *When Fred was a Grey, did he contact humans?*

F: Yes, he worked with, and was a part of the hybridization program.

S: What was that like?

F: It was not fun for him. He did not enjoy scaring people. No matter how hard he tried, even though he was not trying to scare them, they would be scared when they were contacted.

S: What was Fred's role amongst the Greys?

F: He was a worker who received instructions from the leader.

S: What was his day-to-day life like as a Grey? Did he eat?

F: There was a little cube of something that was nutrient dense to keep the body from disintegrating and breaking down that was eaten.

This was very confirming information and matched up with the information that Chris shared in his session.

S: What does it feel like to be a Grey; do you have any feelings, or none at all?

F: They don't have much feeling. I could tell certain things weren't right, but I couldn't tell what I was experiencing because Greys don't necessarily have an emotional computation. But I was able to empathize. There was an exchange and a very cold response.

S: Did you have a real body or use an avatar body?

F: I had an avatar body.

S: What was that like? How did it feel?

F: They have the body prepared for the soul first. The avatar suits look almost like these tubes laid out inside of the ship. The bodies are selected by a machine, and the machine looks like balls of orbs spinning inside of it until there is a signal flash indicating that the suit is selected. Then it draws that soul and conscious memory into the vessel, into the avatar suit. The vessel, the suit, is powered by the soul's energy.

S: *Could you feel outside of the suit? Does it feel like skin when you wear the body?*

F: It feels like the same texture of a dolphin or porpoise's skin.

S: *What is it like to wear it?*

F: It feels comfortable, but also machine-like to me.

S: *Why that design? Why is it Grey?*

F: I forgot all of this, but wow, it's very efficient and it's more versatile than I remembered. I used it better and faster. It's small but allows me to get into tight places. I can hide with this suit. It's compact and is more of a fibrous material with that dolphin skin structure on the outside, but that fibrous build on the inside is very strong. It has incredible strength.

S: *What is your home like as a Grey? Where do you live?*

F: It is a large ship out in space, it doesn't look like it even has walls, and there is a gigantic glowing ball in the middle of this structure that looks like soul energy. This is the mother ship, a place where other ships come from.

S: *Is there any light there?*

F: It's dark, it doesn't seem bright to me, but I can see stars in the distance. This is a very artificial world that I live in. This is where I live as a Grey extra-terrestrial.

S: *Does the ship ever move, or does it stay there?*

F: It's stationary. Ships come and go from this mother ship.

S: *What are the ships like that come and go?*

F: I see a lot of big and smaller cigar-shaped crafts, and there are some disk-shaped crafts that come in and out of these cigar-shaped crafts. They look like massive, long spherical cigar-shaped ships.

S: *How did that lifetime end?*

F: Every Grey extra-terrestrial lifetime, unless they are killed by a human, ends by choice when you would like to end it. You just leave your body and ask them to put your soul back into the sphere within the mother ship or move you somewhere else. Sometimes you can ask to be shot out into the universe and recycled, or whatever it is that you choose.

S: *If they are future versions of us, what do they want us to know about the new technology?*

F: It's not that they don't want us to evolve with our technology, they have been giving us the technology, but they want us to do it the right way where we don't lose our emotions. They need people to understand who the Grey extra-terrestrials really are, to not fear them, and to not kill them. They want us all to come together.

S: **When Earth and the humans on it achieve this ascension, will the Grey alien race disappear if they are the future versions of us?**

F: Yes, but only for some timelines and futures. Not everyone will follow this ascension path. There is always room for the Greys.

S: *When you were out in space and could see Earth, what is the shape of the Earth? Is it flat or spherical?*

F: It can be either depending on the collective's belief system.

S: *Why do some people claim that it is flat?*

F: Because in a sense it is! This hologram reality looks like a 3-D rendering program where you have an empty space with a flat floor and that flat floor is just mesh. When you put a shape in there, that is where you get your 3-D image. You can put a sphere in the center of all of this and it will be on a flat floor. The rendering goes on forever as endless and flat. So, when we call this a realm, technically this could also be an endless plane because we are walking around and rendering it through the programs on Earth to think that it is a ball. The shape of the Earth is really generated by every living thing experiencing it. If we were told from the beginning that we lived on a cube and we all agreed upon it, then that is what it would be.

S: *What shape do people consider Earth in the future?*

F: They consider it more of a realm in the future than something with a shape. Imagine a bubble under water and if you had just the right amount of refraction of light to see underneath the bubble, you might see colors or shapes. From the perspective of looking at Earth from space, it could be round, could be a sphere, but really when you go into the atmosphere it could be anything. It might just be a never-ending flat surface, but you can only see so far or render so much of it. **The potential for the shape and possibilities of Earth are limitless** and they are all valid, and yet another tool to divide humans. The Earth could also act as a geocentric universe rather than a heliocentric one where everything revolves around the Earth instead. If one were to perceive it this way, it's actually a more beautiful pattern of planets in that the patterns of the planets form a flower shape.

S: *What do you mean by that?*

F: For those who perceive the Earth and planets to be geocentric, in order to compensate for the retrograde of mercury, the orbital path would loop and that would create flower shapes when viewed.

S: *Is there anything about Venus that you could tell me?*

F: Venus is mysterious. They are an underground civilization where they don't live on the surface of their planet. They travel on it with their suits and their crafts, but they live underground. They have influence here on Earth, especially within our government.

S: *Why?*

F: They have worked with our government for a very long time. The people on Venus are very Earthly looking. They look like humans; they have human shapes and human features.

S: *What is their life like there?*

F: Very similar to Earth, but there is a large population of artificial intelligence there.

S: *What do they do there?*

F: They are very much like us, but their society is structured differently. Individual jobs are solely based on skill, and everyone does not learn the same things like they do here. They are very interested in genetic experimentation whereas humans on Earth are more reluctant. They are more refined and more advanced as far as technology.

S: *Do the Greys have a planet now?*

F: The Greys have a base now, but not a home planet that is fully ready.

S: *Tell me more.*

F: The Greys use moons and planets that are hollowed out in a glassblowing sort of fashion and the Greys will use them as a base. These moons and planets are great ways for the Greys to travel and stay hidden. The Greys do have a planet that is beginning its new life. It was greatly damaged in the war with the Ebens. As we have said before, the Greys are a space group now and have been for a long time. One planet of origin for the Greys was within the Zeta system. It's possible that it is uninhabitable at this time, but their original home planet is also Earth. The Greys are a time traveling species who have altered timelines and therefore have multiple origins at this point. However, humans are their past and future, which makes the Earth another planet of origin.

S: *Tell me more about the Greys. Do they have souls if they have lost their emotions?*

F: Yes, they have souls, and they are different from artificial intelligence. They do use artificial intelligence a lot though and have robots that work with them that are artificial intelligence as well. The Greys do appear as if they are artificial intelligence, but they are not.

Below is a short segment of another interesting session about artificial intelligence and the Greys:

Kim's session:

K: It's dark inside and I'm wearing a uniform that is very close to the skin. It looks navy or black. This uniform is important; you have to wear this to live here.

S: *What is this uniform like?*

K: The uniform provides you with everything, everything that you need to survive here. It's very interesting!

S: *What does it look like where you are?*

K: It's very dark, and very sterile. Everyone I see around me looks the same, exactly the same.

S: *What do you mean?*

K: We are clones, robots! Everyone is built the same. We do not have an organic consciousness, but an artificial intelligence.

S: *Do you have skin under your uniform?*

K: I don't see any skin. I have gloves, we aren't human. My body feels very thin. We're all lined up almost like an army inside a craft of some sort.

S: *What do you do there?*

K: We stand in waiting, waiting for orders. We are sent on different missions.

S: *Do you have emotions or thoughts?*

K: No. We don't have any emotions; we just wait for orders to do something. Nothing is exciting or interesting. There's no satisfaction when there are no emotions. We are fully robotic.

S: *Do you sleep or eat?*

K: No, nothing is needed, however you must stay in the uniform. The uniform allows you to function.

S: *What does this craft that you're on look like?*

K: It looks like very sterile stainless steel. Nobody sits, we just stand there. There are no windows. There is a voice that speaks to us over a speaker system who gives us orders, but we don't see the person who does this.

S: *What does the voice sound like?*

K: It's very monotone and instructional.

S: *Tell me about some of the missions that you have been on.*

K: We have been sent to protect and be the first line of defense in case of invasions on other planets.

S: *Did you ever see the beings that you were defending?*

K: One time I saw that we were protecting beings, they didn't look human. They lived inside what looked like a hollowed-out moon. I always stayed on the outside to protect, but I saw that there were plants inside this place. We never went inside; we only stayed outside to protect the outside. There were beings that wanted to invade this place.

S: *What were the inhabitants like?*

K: They were Grey extra-terrestrials. The Grey extra-terrestrials needed protection and our help to defend them, but after a time they didn't want us there anymore and thought that they could handle whatever was happening on their own.

S: *What happened next?*

K: When we were no longer needed, they phased out our missions.

S: *What happened to that place that you were guarding?*

K: The Grey extra-terrestrials are still there trying to rebuild that planet.

S: *What happened after you left?*

K: We were turned off. It didn't feel like anything to be turned off. There was no emotional attachment, but my soul went back to floating through the stars and that felt like a huge relief. I chose to have a life as a robot to experience disconnection, but now I'm happy to just be, and to be restored. I feel free and light and relaxed just to be.

CHAPTER 17:
ARRIVING ON THE NEW LAND

I worked with Les to find out the culmination of the Trail. I was curious to see how it all unfolded and what it was really like when they arrived in Oklahoma.

S: How did your tribe handle it when you first arrived at the new land?

L: It was very strange because we had passed all kinds of fertile land while we walked and then we made it to this barren, dry, and hot area of land and they told us that this was ours now. The new land was flat, and we didn't know how to live in an area like this. We still learned how to survive even though it was difficult. It was hard to find a water source at first because we didn't know these new lands. Some of us went to look for water and it took days. We were all so tired and malnourished, and the new land was so hot and dry which made the lack of water worse. I remember taking my wolf with me and walking for what seemed like forever, looking for water. I could feel the weight of my legs as if I was almost dragging myself. I was so exhausted by the time that we found the right water source that the first thing I did was fall into it and drink as much as I could. I had these leather bags that I had made from deer and boar skin that I filled with the water, and I strapped them on my wolf's back to carry them back to the tribe. At first, we had to ration the water until we all migrated to this area. Since we would go and fetch water for people daily, it made it easier for us to map the land out.

S: What else did you notice about the new land?

L: There was this red clay everywhere and not many trees to bring us shade. We had to make houses out of mud.

S: *Did you lose a lot of people on the Trail of Tears?*

L: So many, too many. Most of our elders passed away and that left only us to carry the stories but not all our people had been properly trained in the time that we had. It would normally take until a person was elderly to understand this wisdom and to have all this knowledge. We lost a lot of our stories, but the ones we remembered we held onto. We did the most we could with what we had to try to preserve what culture we had left.

S: *After you moved to the water source, what happened?*

L: Life was hard because the water wasn't at all like the mountain water that we were used to. Instead of it flowing downstream, it was flat water. It tasted different and it had different minerals that our bodies had to adapt to. The minerals were so different from what our bodies were genetically made to be drinking. We were designed to drink the water that was on our old lands, but this new water caused most of us discomfort as we tried to adjust to it.

S: *Tell me more.*

L: The water had different bacteria in it that caused stomach issues and people would eventually turn to alcohol to help with the pain, but this made the situation worse.

S: *Where did they get alcohol?*

L: They could go into the town nearby, but it was a dangerous place to be. Some people were somewhat kind to us, and they showed us how to make certain things from wheat, like alcohol. To me this concoction tasted terrible, and it made everything go dizzy. But some of my people loved it because it was a temporary *escape from the pain they were experiencing.*

S: *Was there anger after having been moved? How did your people handle it?*

L: It was hard. There was great anger and sorrow that was so fierce and powerful that it built up in the DNA and affected the generations to come.

S: *Tell me more about that.*

L: There is still a lot of depression that runs in family lines that directly derives from this, and it has caused so many casualties because there is such a heaviness and denseness of the feelings that went with walking the Trail. For many of my people it is like a cloud making almost like an atmospheric bubble of dense energy. I want my people to realize that they are not the dense energy that they are holding onto. It is right to feel the feelings because it is a terrible thing that occurred. However, there is a way to heal that and move with it. Realize that you are so much bigger than what those people made you feel you were.

S: *Tell me more about the new land.*

L: It was many moons after we arrived at the water source and settled into the disappointment and trauma of what had occurred to our people that the numbness started to recede. At first the shock had placed almost like a film over our grief but as this disappeared, we had to process what we had just been through.

S: *What happened with the woman you loved? Did she make it to the new land with you?*

L: I had given up my dreams of ever finding love with the woman that I was in love with. I stopped pursuing her until one night, months later, she asked me if I wanted to take a night walk.

S: *What happened?*

L: We walked under the stars, and we talked about our future and what was to come, but it wasn't like the old night walks. There was an undeniable heaviness to our lives now. I remember that she just started crying and crying and I didn't know what to do except just hold her. I remember that I didn't know what to say and years later she still makes fun of me about that, but I held her for what felt like days while she cried and cried and when she finally stopped crying, she kissed me. I had forgotten that feeling for so long, the magic of her touch, and I felt how her kiss instantly brought me back to life. I had dreamt of her lips and her touch for so long that I felt like I was in one of my dreams! She said that she loved me and that she wanted to be with me.

S: *What happened next?*

L: We decided to have a ceremony to celebrate. We both thought it would bring happiness to a bleak situation.

S: *What was your ceremony like?*

L: I will never forget it. I wore a beautiful wolf skin. It made me very emotional as it was the pelt of one of our oldest tribal wolf friends. Wearing the pelt was a way of honoring the past and celebrating our future. We would always keep the pelts of our wolves that would pass away and use them for special ceremonies because these animals were so special to us. Since the wolf was the chosen animal for our tribe, we used the wolf pelt around our shoulders but wore deer skin clothing as well. The deer skin would be made specifically for this ceremony, with intricate beading that was made by using berries to dye it. We would first carve these beads out of wood and paint them with berries to give them their color.

S: *What did the design look like?*

L: There was a phoenix design across my chest but the wolf pelt around my shoulders was not made into a design.

S: *What did she wear?*

L: She had something like a shawl and a wolf pelt on her shoulders as well, but the shawl had a big intricate design on the back of it and it went down to the back of her calves.

S: *What did the design on her back look like?*

L: It looks like a phoenix and a sun.

S: *Was there a meaning for this design?*

L: I'm trying to remember; the phoenix was a symbol of the grandfather, and the sun is a portal. We believed that it was the hole that the Sky Woman came from and so the phoenix is flying towards the sun as a way of showing enlightenment.

S: *What was the ceremony like? Can you tell me about it?*

L: (Les started to cry) She looked so beautiful. I had had brief glimpses of the feeling of oneness before, flashes of it in meditation, but during the ceremony when we joined our hands together and walked in a circle around the fire, I felt that oneness with another person for the first time in my life.

S: *Tell me more.*

L: It was the best moment of my life. There was a lot of laughter. We danced around the fire, ate lots of food and told many jokes.

S: *Did you ever have children together or no?*

L: We did. We ended up having four beautiful children of our own, but I always felt that I had twenty or thirty because we all did our part to take care of all the children.

CHAPTER 18:
UNDERSTANDING THE NEW ENERGY

Below is a session with Yana who in her session talks about the importance of connecting with the Earth and the new energy.

Y: The indigenous cultures remind us to attune to the Earth.

S: *Tell me more.*

Y: It's important to understand the subtle energies available now. If we don't attune ourselves to these subtleties within our field, and open our sensitivity, then we will not receive that higher light source that is coming from the center of the Earth. There is a lot of high frequency energy that is being pumped from the center of the Earth right now and if we are not attuned to it, not using it, and not in harmony with it, then we can't use it.

S: *Are people in disharmony with this light?*

Y: Many are when they are in fear. When they are in fear they are cut off from the Earth and from their body. When humans are in the state of fear there is a lack of awareness of what they are. We are resisting this energy and that creates complications.

S: *Is there a way to accept this energy?*

Y: Pay attention to the subtleties within your body because that will help you to attune to the Earth's body.

S: *What would that feel like for a person?*

Y: It feels like feeling and sensing things that you wouldn't normally experience, and humans need to understand that this is new. Humans don't even have the words yet for these new subtleties available because they are brand new. We say to start by just noticing without judgment. Noticing the subtleties is a powerful thing because it brings this into this reality. Noticing anchors information into this realm. So, the more you notice, the more you are anchoring more information into this reality and the more information you gather, the more your mind can do something with it. The fourth dimension is already here.

S: *Are we moving into this different dimension, a fourth dimension?*

Y: That dimension is already accessible.

S: *How do you access it?*

Y: You access it by connecting to what is actually here rather than what you are told or programed to believe. If you want to access more of this new intelligent energy, then you can't hold on to the past and your old beliefs and ideas because that cuts you off from what is actually here. What is here is brand new and you need to make yourselves available and attuned to it because many of you are still stuck in the past due to your attachment to your mind and your thoughts.

S: *So, what do we need to do?*

Y: By being present you can access more information rather than getting stuck in your thoughts which are based on the past. Humans need to give their minds the information that is available to them now.

S: *What information is available?*

Y: A way to communicate with the Earth and the environment in a seamless way. Humans can communicate with their environment and start understanding that the Earth is very intelligent and can tell you ways to do things efficiently. Learn to start asking the Earth in terms of energy, resources, livelihood, where to build things, where to live. Communicating with the Earth is available to you now and will prove incredibly valuable in your future. Developing the sensitivity to communicate with nature, animals and the Earth in a way that is harmonious is your future and your sciences will start to develop along these lines. Those who are more attuned to the Earth will flourish. Industries not in line with this evolution will crumble further. They will suffer.

S: *Why?*

Y: **There is a lot of suffering when one doesn't attune to what is**. Suffering is largely taking place due to thoughts and beliefs. Many are operating in a fear-based belief system and going against what is becoming stronger and stronger here, which is the Earth's consciousness and what works for the Earth.

S: *So, the Earth's consciousness is getting stronger? Why is it getting stronger now?*

Y: This is an ascension process of light and expansion for all in this realm and Earth is experiencing this too. Those who aren't attuned to the process are in direct resistance to it, and resistance creates suffering.

S: *Who am I speaking with?*

Y: We are a group that assists with the ascension. We've come from other Earth systems that have this same consciousness that Earth does.

S: *What do you mean when you say the same consciousness as the Earth?*

Y: There are other Earth planets that have this type of consciousness, almost like a personality. There are many planetary systems, and this Earth is one of many.

S: *Why do you assist with the ascension?*

Y: There is a specific kind of bliss that is produced through the ascension on Earthly planets, a harmony that is very beautiful. And it produces a beauty that I love. And that brings me joy. This is what drives me.

S: *So, you help with the ascension on not only this Earth but other Earths?*

Y: Yes, I started thirteen planets ago.

S: *What was the last planet you helped?*

Y: Mars was the last planet before this one. However, there was a lot of trauma, and some of those memories are still pretty new for me so they are hard to talk about.

S: *Would you tell me more about this?*

Y: Earth needed to be a home for those that didn't make it on Mars. There was a transfer for some of the beings on Mars to go to Earth and I was involved in this. There were also some mistakes made. There was an aggression that was brought to Earth, and this should have been filtered more.

S: *How did it get brought to Earth?*

Y: We knew that we wouldn't filter completely what came to Earth and we always knew that there would be a period when the energy would have to sort itself out. There were many foreign energies that were brought in that created turmoil and chaos. We did what we could to ease the process, but I witnessed a lot of suffering.

S: *What did you see?*

Y: Agony, hell on Earth. I witnessed it. An incredible amount of love is needed to witness this much pain and ignorance.

S: *What was that like?*

Y: I had empathy for the survivors of Mars as they had to learn the hard way on Earth and experience a lot of darkness.

S: *Why?*

Y: It was just part of the process of evolution in this system. Because of diversity of consciousness and different levels of beings all in one planet, there is a lot of conflict because of belief. Belief is the single most potent cause of conflict on these Earthly planets.

S: *Tell me more.*

Y: A planet that is experiencing turmoil is easier to take advantage of.

S: *When the beings from Mars were transferred, what was that like?*

Y: It was horrible and messy and didn't go well. There was too much destructive energy that tipped the scales. A portal was opened that allowed them to get from there to here. They were immediately placed into the center of the Earth, then later brought to the surface. Some incarnated in human form. Some didn't. There were many different types of beings on Earth at this time. Humans were the minority at this point. There were highly evolved creatures here, large creatures as well. There was a period when there were second density beings with other evolved beings here at the same time. Then evolution took over with natural selection. Expansion is never easy and involves an expansion of your belief systems. Old beliefs needed to be replaced with new ones. This was a long process.

S: *What was the belief system that needed to change?*

Y: The knowledge that you are more than just the physical aspect, that you are spirit, that knowledge needed to be anchored. One of the biggest beliefs that limit humans now is the reliance on their minds when they need to embrace their heart and live in the heart. The knowing within goes beyond thoughts, beyond the deeper wisdom. You need to trust that wisdom now in order to evolve. This is a crossing point and a leap of faith.

S: *How long do people have to do this?*

Y: There is no time limit. The more you resist the heart energy, the more it will pile up. As one human starts to register these new subtle energies and has an experience, then it becomes available to everyone as we are each helping to activate this collectively.

S: *All you have to do is be aware and notice?*

Y: Yes. Attune yourself to the Earth and notice. As you notice the subtleties you will start to download information and then the intellect will start to notice. So, gather information from the surroundings, including your body. Just gather information through your body and heart. There is a bliss energy from the sun that helps humans to stabilize this energy. The more you can absorb the sun the more you can help your energy field.

S: *Are people experiencing this differently according to how much sun they receive in their area, or no?*

Y: Yes, there are certain areas where this energy is more stable because it has held it longer. We are building ourselves up to hold more joy because we are not used to that energy. This higher frequency coming from the sun is helping all.

S: *Is there a way to tell if you lived on Mars and are reincarnated as a human now?*

Y: If you have the wisdom of understanding what Earth needs, you were most likely on Mars because you've had the experience of the devastation before. Those who were on Mars learned a great deal because they saw directly the cause of the devastation there and how those behaviors caused the same devastation here with the indigenous cultures.

S: *Is there any advice you would like to give humans?*

Y: Don't grow weary, it will be ok. All your hard work is paying off, finally now. Appreciate the moment and be in gratitude. Trust. There are a lot of powerful energies that are being synchronized now, so be ready.

Below is another session with Fred to gain more perspective.

F: There are many stuck souls still on the Trail of Tears who have not been able to cross over.

S: *Tell me more about that.*

F: There is one woman I see with a blanket who is stuck there, unable to cross over and obtain closure.

S: *Why is she stuck?*

F: She separated herself out of grief. These souls are looking for an Earthly solution to a spiritual problem and they become stuck in a cycle. They get stuck in the same path over and over again.

S: *What solution do they need?*

F: Souls like this need confirmation from the humans that are incarnated here. That way they know from this Earthly realm that they are no longer alive and that it's ok to move on.

S: *Can you still incarnate in a body while a part of you is stuck? How does that work?*

F: Soul splitting from severe unhealed soul trauma happens all the time for humans.

S: *How does that affect the human?*

F: A lot of people will feel a generational anger, anxiety, sadness, or always feeling like they are missing something and never truly able to find happiness.

S: *Is there anything that can help a group of people like that?*

F: For the people here, that are missing this piece of their soul, many will be drawn to this book. Reading this book will help them understand this trauma connection without them necessarily having to go through the memories. These stuck souls are all there waiting on the other side. There's many of them standing there. They are just watching and waiting for their human incarnation to read something like this and are just waiting to see the healing happen. When humans heal in the physical, those souls will find themselves again. They will be recharged and reconnected with the part of them that was stuck.

S: *Why does this keep happening? I've heard there's also stuck souls in Atlantis and Lemuria.*

F: If you don't learn the lessons, it gets more severe and deeper each time. It's all meant to be one big trigger in the now and recognizing that all these past traumas are our own doing. They are experiences and nothing more. In the now is where we can fix the past and the future just by coming back together and loving and living with the purpose of undoing the things that have been done.

S: *Tell me more.*

F: The joy of this is the rediscovery of all of it again. So, we don't wish to spoil it. This is the past. It's a dream within a dream. You are all just remembering. When you see a Star being that comes down and talks to you, most likely that is you in the future. It is already there. You are seeing yourself in a higher form that already exists. So, it knows where you are on your evolution and when you see this higher version of you, you are also already over there consoling yourself from beyond where you are now. You are dipping down in your own meditation in a realm far beyond here.

S: *So, are we dipping down into a meditation right now?*

F: Yes. We are in Source's dream. It is all a memory. We are floating around in everything and nothing all at once. We're just experiencing a little bit of an echo from the past because the transition is so wonderful.

S: *What can we do during this transition time?*

F: Remember the old ways. The spiritual ways, the connection to the Earth. Remember that you are not separate from your environment. Without your environment you wouldn't exist. Once you remember that and you get others to remember and unite, that is how you heal, and heal the past. This doesn't just include humans it includes beings from higher realms and other worlds that have helped us and watched us and guided us this whole time. And all the animals that we see. Everyone matters.

S: *I'm so curious about the wisdom of the Earth. I've heard there is a powerful plant that the Egyptians used to make into a tea.*

F: The Blue Lotus flower. It is medicinal, but there is a lotus flower under the Great pyramid that is centered on the Flower of Life grid underneath. It shoots a beam into space.

S: *Tell me more about that.*

F: Deep down underneath the pyramid is an energetic Blue Lotus with a beam that comes up though the pyramid, but it is supposed to be hitting a crystal that goes out into the universe through the top of the pyramid. It is not only supposed to go into the universe but also downwards into the center of the Earth as well.

S: *What was the point of that energetic grid?*

F: It was set up in the pyramid so that one could meditate and send oneself out into the astral realm with ease in order to receive information from the cosmos and the Earth at the same time. That was one of the uses of it. That was also how beings could use the pyramids to communicate with other worlds, similar to the Sphinx. The energy sensor is in the shape of a Blue Lotus flower that is spinning.

S: *Why is the Blue Lotus so important?*

F: These vibrations from the energy create the Blue Lotus shape. This shape is a symbol that reminds us of the natural force that we have, that we can use to exist. The Egyptian Blue Lotus tea is very powerful and contains intelligence from the flower that when ingested brings the intelligence of the plant to the humans.

S: *What about Cannabis? I've heard it is also has intelligence and a consciousness?*

F: Yes, that is correct. Cannabis was brought to Earth by the Star People and shown to humans for its medicinal purposes as was other psychedelic plants. Cannabis has a strong intelligent energetic field. You don't have to use the plant to align with the strong light frequency of that plant. The resonance of that plant is love.

S: *Is there anything about Hemp that is interesting?*

F: Hemp is the way of the future. It makes concrete that petrifies over time and removes the carbon footprint.

S: *Why did the Hopi say that there will be a blue star that will fall that is manmade?*

F: The blue star that may fall is a space station. There are more than just one or two space stations floating around Earth. Many don't realize the size of the objects in the sky as well as their distance. Often when you see a ball of light flying around it is actually a humongous object and not a tiny satellite reflecting a small amount of light. There are many different space stations that have been put up over the years through secretive contracted work with rocket companies. A lot of times the people sending these things up in the sky don't even know what they are sending up there. There are a lot of satellites as well as ancient satellites and wreckage up there as well. The Hopi saw a potential for one to fall and crash onto Earth, but there are many different potentials and timelines, and this might not even happen at this point.

S: *Are we in the Fourth World?*

F: We are entering the Fifth World, but we are already going through the fourth dimension to enter the golden age, which will be a Fourth/ Fifth world blend. The Fourth World is the fourth dimension where we are manifesting faster. But we are leaving that Fourth World. The new age is coming.

S: *Right now, we are living in the fourth dimension?*

F: Yes, many are and that is why everything is chaotic for some.

S: *What makes the fourth dimension different?*

F: Manifestation is faster. If you are in-tune with the Earth, you will be able to see a shimmer between objects and the air around you will be a little more visible. You will start seeing brighter colors. You will start seeing people's aura. You will be able to see their energy as well.

S: *What about the people who are not attuned to this?*

F: They might feel anxious. The fourth density is really a manifestation realm where it is all happening faster. However, those in fear are also getting more fearful because manifestation is strong right now. So now is the moment to pick your side because as we leave the fourth density and hit the fifth that is where you will stay.

S: *Tell me more.*

F: All of your lifetimes and timelines are merging. Each individual person is merging with their other lifetimes at an exponential rate and that is why people feel as if they are clearing other lifetimes, because they are. Some people are releasing so much trauma that they are becoming lighter. Humans are slowly starting to become themselves. Earth is a very important place for a lot of reasons, but mostly because Earth is the school of enlightenment.

Below is another session with Yana

S: *Could you scan Yana's body and tell me how Yana's body is looking?*

Y: Her body looks fine. There are no issues except for the throat chakra, there is fear in that chakra from not speaking her truth or expressing her authenticity, but if she releases this, she will be fully ready for her mission.

S: *Could you release it now? Or is there anything else that you want her to understand about this?*

Y: It is trauma from her past and she needs to notice whenever she is remembering traumatic memories, accompanied by feelings of sorrow. What is happening is that we are bringing these memories and feelings to her attention so that she can release the wounds from her past. Just by witnessing the sorrow inside of her body is enough to release the memories from her body as well.

S: *So just by witnessing the sorrow will release these memories from her body?*

Y: Yes. In a sense, Yana is the one who is choosing to hold on to her fear. And so, we cannot alter her freewill. She needs to be aware that she is hanging on to the past needlessly.

S: *Now she's aware of this, is there anything else that you need her to understand?*

Y: We are trying to show her that being her authentic self is the greatest service she can provide for herself and for people. People need her authenticity, and we are showing her this every day through her interactions with others. In this way she can understand her role and her value. She is now aware that it is purely her own choosing to allow this fear to stand in the way.

S: *Now that she got this message, can you release this fear for her now?*

Y: Yes. We will begin the process. She will begin to feel a lightness in the throat as we release this fear. The tightness that she has been feeling there is gone now.

S: *Is there anything else you want to tell her?*

Y: Just to recognize that she is connected to the Divine Self. She's always connected to us, to her higher self, and so she does not need to fear anything. She does not need to fear making any mistakes or doing anything wrong. We are guiding her every moment.

S: *How do you go about communicating with her? Does she hear you? Does she sense you, or just know things?*

Y: We pour information through her crown chakra. It feels like a tingly sensation right at the top of her head when we are trying to get her attention. When she feels this sensation, this heat, right at the top of her head she should understand that we are sending her messages and that she needs to pay attention.

S: *Will she get these messages consciously, or not?*

Y: Consciously. They will show up as inspired images and thoughts in her mind and she will know when she receives them. The more she pays attention to those intuitive thoughts, those intuitive hunches, the more quickly they will be coming in.

S: *Who communicates with Yana?*

Y: It would depend on the situation, but most of those who communicate with Yana are different aspects of her soul speaking to her. She has a large network that she's connected to, both here on Earth and on different planets.

S: *When a person has an oversoul and they're connected to all these different parts, do the different parts have different agendas, or do they continue with the same agenda?*

Y: They all have the same purpose and agenda. The different aspects of the soul and the different bodies that house the different aspects each have their own personality flavor, but their goal is unified.

S: *What is the agenda for Yana's oversoul?*

Y: It is to assist the awakening of souls; it is to assist in the ascension process.

S: *How do the versions of Yana assist with this?*

Y: It would depend on what planet they're on. Earth has a very specific program. For Earth, the program is to release memory. To release the past.

S: *Why is that the program for Earth? Why do we come in with all of these traumas and memories and then try to release them? What is this all about?*

Y: On Earth, human beings learn through storytelling. Their consciousness evolves through experiencing different stories, different versions of themselves. This is part of the joy of Earth, to be immersed in these stories and to learn about God through these stories, and so they must embody these stories to learn. And once that learning process is complete, all memory, all story is released.

S: *What does that feel like? What is that like for a person if they can release their story, if they complete this?*

Y: **It is the greatest release that a soul can attain before they merge back into union with God. It's the greatest release, to release the illusion of who they thought they were.**

S: *How do you go about doing that? Is there an easy way?*

Y: The way is becoming easier for those who want it. Now on Earth, the energy is ripe for this type of release. It depends on the individual and how much each individual is ready to remember. Are they ready to remember that the past versions of themselves here on Earth were only illusions?

S: *What do you mean by saying that those versions are only illusions? Can you tell me more about that?*

Y: They are only illusions showing us the stages of fear we had to go through. It is all about releasing fear, releasing fear-based beliefs. We had to go through this process because there is no need to be afraid, there is no need to wear such small ideas about who you are. It was just part of this process. But humans have hung on for far too long. This process has been repeating itself for far too long.

S: *Why has this been going on so long?*

Y: Because of how strong this programming is, how strong the amnesia is.

S: *Why is it so strong?*

Y: There are different reasons for this. Human consciousness has also been tampered with on this planet. And so, there was an incentive for certain beings to prolong this amnesia process. Because if humans were to remember, they could not be controlled any longer.

S: *Who are humans really?*

Y: Human beings are not what they originally were. It's very hard to pin down the identity of a human being because of how mixed they are. Their genetics are mixed with the DNA of so many Star People. Human beings are an experiment. They are beings whose lives are for the purpose of this experimentation with consciousness. Any being can get attracted here and inhabit a human body and **the Earth has become largely an experimentation project for the evolution of consciousness.**

S: *So, all souls that come here are just part of the experiment. They know that coming in?*

Y: Yes, all souls that are here come here for this purpose. In the past there were purely Earth based beings, but they do not exist anymore here because interbreeding has been so prolific.

S: *Why?*

Y: There are several reasons for this and there were some errors early on with the first colonizers of the Star Seed beings on this planet. They interbred very quickly with the humans, and this caused a lot of problems in the very beginning. But since then, Earth has been positioned to be a place for these types of interbreeding to occur.

S: *Is there a purpose for all the interbreeding?*

Y: Absolutely. The purpose of this interbreeding is to understand unity on a grand scale. What we have seen is that no matter where the DNA comes from, when DNA from different realms and different dimensions come together, they are always still acting for the same singular goal. Which means consciousness is unified.

S: *What is the agenda for consciousness?*

Y: The agenda is to understand that no matter where you are on the scale of awareness or the illusion of separation and no matter how far you are from God, you have the equal opportunity to access that unity consciousness, that remembering.

S: *How do they access it?*

Y: That has been a big part of the experimentation here to understand the mechanics of this process, and what we have understood is that it is through emotion that we access that mechanism for remembering. Take the feeling of fear for example. If one can truly access that fear to its core and the essence of that fear, then they can unlock the memory within it, transmute it, and access that unification that comes from doing this.

S: *All you have to do is follow your emotions to their core?*

Y: Yes, by following the integrity of the emotion without any judgment. That will unlock memory within your DNA and the memory of unification. But this practice is not necessarily understood on Earth at this time.

S: *Is this practice understood in other places?*

Y: Yes, it is. What happens on Earth greatly contributes to the understanding of this process and then it is used in other realms. On Earth there is resistance because of the conditioning that awakening cannot happen that quickly, but we have found that certain techniques do allow for a certain speed in that ascension process.

S: *What type of techniques?*

Y: This is brand new information, and we feel it may be confusing to some so we will find the best way to describe these techniques that bypass any form of conditioning. This is done through the human's emotions, and it involves the energy of feeling. Emotions are a gateway through the universe and a perfectly intact replica of God and unity. It is a perfect replica of that unity because, for example, if you could visualize emotions like a string, and on one side of that string is abject terror, which is like the equivalent of hell, and on the other side of that string is ecstatic bliss, then you will see that abject terror meets perfectly with bliss. It forms a perfect circle. So, if you follow that terror, just the integrity of the feeling itself will bring you to that bliss, if you do not hold on to any resistance. People do not like fear. They do not like to experience the depths of abject terror. It's not considered a good thing. But if one were to sit deeply and utterly with that feeling, without any resistance whatsoever, if one were so lucky as to have that fear come alive inside of them, and if they were to feel it and to be with it, and to follow it to its depths, then it would take them almost instantaneously to complete and utter bliss.

S: *So, if you follow completely the feeling, it will lead you to Source basically?*

Y: Yes.

S: *Is there any advice on how a person can start to do that?*

Y: One could take an existing fear and sit with it. If you were to feel that fear in your body and to truly be with it, that fear will take you deeper and deeper into it, which means it will take you closer and closer into that unity.

S: *What about a positive emotion? Can you do the same with feeling good? Or does that lead you to the opposite emotion?*

Y: There are many techniques that use positive emotions, but the technique that I would like to share with humans now is one that uses negative emotions because the dynamics of Earth are still playing within that duality realm. And so, if you were to do this with a positive feeling, it may or may not have the reverse effect or it may induce fear if you were to start with joy. So, we are showing a technique for releasing these negative emotions in order to bring you to the other side of the illusion.

S: *So, essentially these emotions are helping humans to wake up then. So, these negative emotions and our collective trauma are actually tools?*

Y: Yes, these are absolutely tools. They are tools that are also used to prevent awakening. But what we are trying to introduce into collective awareness is that these tools can and will be used for mass awakening once understood.

S: *What do you mean by that? When will they be used for mass awakening?*

Y: When human beings learn how to correctly use their feelings, there will be groups utilizing this technique to assist one another in this awakening process. Right now, human beings find it difficult to allow such feelings of fear to surface. It is too much for the ego, for the frail identity of the human being, because of their conditioning, to allow such emotions to surface. But when certain individuals come to understand this process, they will assist the others.

S: *That's really good to know. Is there anything else about that that you want to say?*

Y: No, it is already unfolding. There's so much effort, so much wisdom, especially the wisdom from the indigenous cultures coming back in many ways and there is nothing now that will stop this.

S: *Why was it suppressed?*

Y: There are many reasons but there are some who are enjoying the current program, the current game, so much that they do not want to release that game. And on this planet, as the Earth consciousness shifts more and more, that game will have to be released because it is no longer congruent with the consciousness of this planet. However, there are those who are invested in that game and so are seeking to prolong it. That is also part of evolution because things cannot happen overnight. So, the process is being moderated. And what is happening is a weeding out process. So, for those beings who are truly invested in this old program, they're coming to a place within themselves where they're acknowledging that they want to stay in that program. And once they acknowledge that, that is their choice. They will leave Earth and they will transfer to a place that is aligned with that program.

S: *What is that program?*

Y: That program is a program of forgetting. They are still getting a benefit from the forgetting. They don't want to remember yet.

S: *What do they get out of this program of not remembering?*

Y: It depends on who you ask. If you're asking Yana, for example, it is very strange to her that one would consciously opt to continue that program because there's much suffering within it. But for these beings, they have not spent enough time in that space of being not God. I mean, for every being, no matter who they are, they all have a seed within them that knows that they are God, and they will never not be God and they are that for eternity. But some would like to experience not being God for a moment.

S: *What is this other place that these people who refuse to wake up go to? Do they die and then are taken to a different place?*

Y: Yes, they die. They're not taken, but their soul gets the chance to do their review and then they will be magnetized to a plane where they feel more comfortable.

S: *What is that plane like? Are there already souls there in this other place?*

Y: These places would be called other Earth-based planets, very, very similar to this one prior to the awakening.

S: *When they leave their body, are they aware they're going to these other Earth-based planets that are like this one? Do these other Earth-based planets have the same type of control, same government style, stuff like that?*

Y: Yes. They have very similar structures. Once these souls that are choosing to leave now, and some are more conscious when they die than others, when they enter in the review process, they will be very much aware of what they're choosing and why. They are completely aware of why they're choosing to prolong that game on another planet.

S: *So, for the people that are staying here that are choosing self-discovery and choosing to awaken, what is happening to them?*

Y: They are merging with God, they are awakening to unity consciousness, they are recognizing that there is no separation between any living being. There is only love, only love exists. And the feelings that are accompanying them are joy, bliss, gratitude, service. These are the things that are happening to these beings more and more.

S: *What about the indigenous cultures?*

Y: It would really depend on which indigenous culture or community you're speaking about, but to give the example of the Native Americans, their trauma can either help them to awaken to unity consciousness, or it can take them to these other planets that I speak of. It would depend on that individual's choice and their stage of awakening. Are they ready to return to unity consciousness or do they need to experience more lives in which they are separate? This is a collective process here on Earth as the planet is moving to her own unity consciousness. There are different things happening now. There are souls who have reached unity consciousness that are choosing to remain here simply to assist with the process. There are souls that once reaching unity consciousness choose to leave this planet to inhabit the higher consciousness planets and the higher consciousness realms. And so, there are many different assignments happening here on Earth.

S: *But why is this all happening now?*

Y: This planet has never collectively awakened before. There have been beings who dwelled on this planet before that were of a much higher consciousness, but the entire planet was not of a higher consciousness yet at that stage. So, the difference now is that every layer of this planet, of this place, of this portal, is now becoming that higher consciousness. Everything now is on the trajectory toward ascension. And unlike before, everything is now being used for that purpose.

S: *What do you mean by that?*

Y: Everything on this planet is now carrying a ripe seed for ascension. So, the nature, the beings, they are on that trajectory of ascending, of reaching that higher consciousness. And so, what is happening is that this is revealing any part of the planet that is not aligned with that trajectory. Anything that is not aligned with the ascension process can be seen as a kind of friction. That is what you are going through right now. The wisdom of the Native Americans is the wisdom of unity consciousness and of respecting the Earth and one another. This information is coming forward because it's very important that people understand these ideas, these concepts, because they need to understand what choice they are making. They need to realize and recognize on every level of their being that they can ascend, that they can choose that unity consciousness, or they can choose separation. Even people who are mired in trauma can use that emotion to ascend and people need to understand that we are no longer in the past, that this is a new realm we are entering, so that they can deliberately and consciously get into that new flow. Hanging on to trauma is the old programming, and so, if they are simply bathing in that trauma and not understanding how to use it, then they will be ushered onto another duality planet to continue that trauma. Even though they do not have to do this, they need to be aware.

S: *Tell me more.*

Y: There has been a lot of extra-terrestrial communication and interaction with higher beings, Star-Seed beings in the area where the Trail of Tears occurred because in a sense, it is part of this experimentation in which we are understanding that trauma and suffering can be used as a fast-track program to ascension.

S: *Why is this happening where the Trail of Tears occurred?*

Y: During the Trail of Tears there was a lot of interaction with extra-terrestrial and Star beings as this was part of a special experimentation project wherein unity conscious was already being reached by many of the members of the indigenous people in that area. There were quite a few who had access to this and there was an interference there as well, a force that wanted to prevent that awakening from taking place.

S: *What type of force?*

Y: A deliberate disruption to that awakening process. In a sense, the humans who walked the Trail of Tears had a very strong connection to the Star beings and they were receiving quite a bit of assistance from them in terms of wisdom. These humans were able to raise their consciousness through this connection that they had and that caught the attention of certain beings who did not want that to spread, who did not want that awakening to happen on a bigger scale. So, there was a deliberate repression, suppression of that awakening and of these indigenous humans. And so, trauma was inflicted upon them. However, I see that on one level this was happening but, on another level, this was simply part of the grand experiment.

S: *Tell me about that.*

Y: Even trauma cannot divert from the ascension process because trauma, all trauma, is the deliberate creation of certain negative feelings. Like we have said negative feelings can be used for the purpose of ascension. And so, **in a sense, there was an experimentation to prove that nothing could really divert ascension happening and that will become a very powerful testimony for the collective.**

S: *So even the trauma inflicted upon the Native Americans couldn't get in the way of ascension.*

Y: Exactly. But now it can be used as a fast track to ascension. So, it can actually help.

S: *How do people know if they walked or lived during this time of the Trail of Tears or if they carry trauma from this?*

Y: They will know because their guides, their higher selves, are triggering that memory. That memory is being activated in order for that trauma release to be a fast track to their ascension. And once they access that unity, they will assist others to do the same. And that is the agreement that they've made.

S: *And what about the Star Seeds that are located on the Trail of Tears? Why are they located there?*

Y: Many Star Seeds choose to live in an area with a strong imprint or strong memory, since that allows more memory to be activated within them. The importance is within the Star Seeds DNA; the DNA is assisting with that trigger.

S: *Can you tell me more about that? What do you mean exactly?*

Y: The activation of DNA sets off an alchemical reaction. Once the Star Seeds within the area begin to remember, and they will remember more quickly because of their Star Seed connections, their DNA becomes activated and then it activates others in that area. Most of the people who are drawn to this area are those who have walked the Trail of Tears before and are the initial human beings that were on the planet here that began this experimentation project. They're very old beings, and therefore, they have the full spectrum of the trauma; they have the full spectrum memory of the trauma inflicted on this planet over and over again. So, they carry the most potent DNA memory, in a sense, because of the breadth of the memory carried within their DNA here on Earth. In this way the activation creates a larger impact, and these people can create a larger activation for the collective because they hold more memory.

S: *Why did the Star People have such a direct communication with the Native Americans?*

Y: They had the most direct communication because they were working together; they began so early in this process together. Native Americans are the human counterpart to the Star Beings that were working here from the beginning.

S: *So, the indigenous cultures were the extra-terrestrial counterpart?*

Y: Yes. They work as a team. They are working together to support this fast-track ascension. They are equally invested in understanding this ascension route, although not all are conscious of this.

S: *When a Native American passes, are they aware of this or no?*

Y: Many are even aware of this before they pass. It depends on the individual. **They may remember extra-terrestrial communication more than other cultures because it was there from the beginning. It is intertwined with them.**

S: *Were they survivors from Lemuria or Atlantis?*

Y: Both. A lot of the beings during that time incarnated on both sides. The reason that incarnation on both sides happened so often was because they were working together towards Earth's ascension without consciously understanding this.

S: *But they both destroyed one another, correct?*

Y: That's correct. They both destroyed one another. However, there is a distinction here between certain kinds of good and evil. They destroyed one another for the purpose of evolution and awakening and understanding. After these civilizations passed, they became aware that they were actually working on the same team because it was important that the destruction occurred for the purpose of this ascension trajectory. Evolution happens in a very funny way, and we have all played many different roles to achieve the current timeline that we are on. When you are a human incarnated in a body you do not realize how much went into this current timeline. A lot of other timelines had to happen in certain ways for it to have finally become distilled into this timeline.

S: *What can help the Native Americans?*

Y: In the next couple hundred years, as the Earth frequency rises, this Earth based frequency will assist with the healing of these indigenous cultures that were destroyed in the process of this evolution. They will get even more help from the Star beings, and they will receive more assistance.

S: *In the next hundred years they will start to receive more assistance?*

Y: Yes. Star beings and humans alike will help with the understanding of how to work with the Native Americans in order to utilize their trauma towards their ascension. So, there will be an extremely big growth spurt for them that will happen. This may not manifest right at this very moment, but it will continue to manifest more and more over the next hundred years.

S: *And what will that look like?*

Y: As the deconditioning process continues here on Earth, in the not-too-distant future, a full disclosure will happen. This means that after that stage of disclosure there will be many Star beings visiting Earth. There will be many Star beings that will not have to use a human disguise to communicate with humans. There will be a lot more Star beings that can openly assist with this healing process. The indigenous communities will be working very closely with the Star beings here on Earth. They won't even need to communicate in dreams or ESP, they will communicate in person.

S: *When do you see that happening?*

Y: I see that happening not in Yana's incarnation now, but in the next one. (Yana is in her thirties in 2022)

S: *What about now? How do you contact extra-terrestrials?*

Y: A lot of extra-terrestrial contact happens during sleep time because the personality of the human being has receded during that time. And the human knows exactly who they're speaking to because it is very clear.

There's no confusion. For some, during the waking time, if they receive messages, they are not sure that they are correct and sometimes their conscious mind interferes. A lot of the messages get lost in translation or lost within the confusion of the ego mind when humans are awake so most communication now happens during sleep time or during deep hypnosis.

S: *Is there anything else that you would like to tell us humans?*

Y: The extra-terrestrials and Native Americans were teaching the same things. One of those things is that Earth's nature kingdom comes from other planets. For example, **mushrooms come to Earth from a different planet in order to teach. These mushrooms show up on Earth as a network and there's a lot of information being shared on Earth at this time from these mushrooms.**

S: *Tell me more.*

Y: They're sharing their sacred wisdom by being here with us. These types of plants are playing a very big role in this ascension process. The plants come from planets that are similar to Earth that have already passed through the ascension phase. So, they are assisting because they already have that pathway mapped out.

S: *And these mushrooms that you're talking about, is that psilocybin or are these just mushrooms?*

Y: I'm seeing that the role of all mushrooms is to create a system to release this plant intelligence. They are spreading and seeding that higher intelligence by being here. The Star People brought them here to Earth.

S: *Do you have to do plant medicine to receive this consciousness or this awareness?*

Y: No, it is not necessary to ingest or do the medicine from the plants, though I am being shown that that is a very potent tool that is available to any who would like to use it for that reason. But these medicines would be best done with the right people. It has to be done with the right people to activate the right type of consciousness within you. Just being around certain trees and places in nature can also activate that consciousness within you, especially if someone is attuning themselves to nature. It is so potent right now at this stage that simply attuning your consciousness is enough to activate that higher consciousness memory. And certain people are being called to move to the places that can activate this consciousness the most.

S: *Is there anything else that you want to say?*

Y: You create the version of Earth that you wish to live on and there are many versions, so choose wisely what you wish to focus on. Whatever you focus on and give your thoughts to, will happen. They cannot not happen. You are creating your reality. The single most important thing to know now is how powerful you all are whether your conditioning allows you to believe it or not.

CHAPTER 19:
MOVING FORWARD

I'm always curious about what my clients experience as they leave their Earthly lives. Below is Aniwaya's account of the final days of such a tragic yet heroic journey.

L: My love passed before me.

S: *Tell me about that.*

L: Her soul's journey was finished. I was upset because I wanted mine to finish at the same time as hers, but I still had more children to teach and more people to speak to.

S: *How did she pass?*

L: She ended up getting sick and left quickly but we both knew that it was going to happen before it happened when she started to decline slightly. At first, I was upset and tried to stop her from leaving me, but she was ready. She was ready to leave this life. She had done all that she came here to do, so I had to put my own feelings aside and recognize that you love someone as much as you are willing to let them go. That is what real love is. Love is not bound by time, and I knew that even though she passed, I could visit her whenever I wanted to. Even though it's not the same, it is still there. Love bridges the gap of what we call time.

S: *How long after she passed did you pass away?*

L: It was about ten years.

S: *How did you know that it was your time to leave?*

L: I knew that I was dying because my mother started coming to me again. She looked like a blue outline of a woman coming up out of the water when she came to me. She hadn't visited me as much since I arrived in this new place. But I knew that death was approaching me because my mother started showing up all the time and when I took my final breath my mother reached for my hand, and I felt myself leave with her.

S: *What did that feel like?*

L: It was exhilarating! It was nothing like anything I had ever felt before. I felt myself leave my body, and the first thing I noticed was a relief from all the aches and pains that I had felt. But not just a relief from that, relief from it all, from the emotional torment that always stays slightly in the back of your mind. I felt relief from it all. And I held my mother's hand as I watched my clan and all that I loved get smaller and smaller in the distance, and then I arrived to where I knew I had been before, the place of light, the oneness. My love was waiting for me on the other side; it was truly amazing.

S: *Was there anything about death that surprised you?*

L: It was what I expected, but then again not at all, because I knew that there was oneness and I had had these moments of that feeling in my life. But to really experience death is different because you can see everything for what it was and why you chose that life for yourself.

S: *Why did you choose that life?*

L: The purpose was to plant the seeds of peace in the world even though there was so much opposition. I see how my life affected everyone I interacted with, even the White Men. I came to experience true love and I fought for peace even if it couldn't be achieved. I came to remember who I was; that was the biggest goal.

S: *What do you mean?*

L: I remembered that my life as Aniwaya was just one blink of what my soul craves to see and experience and so because of that I was able to understand the point of this never-ending experiment which is simply just to experience it all. By choosing this life I knew that it would be difficult, and I thought at times that it was all a failure, that I was a failure. But looking back on my life now I see that this life was anything but. This life turned out exactly the way it was supposed to, and it has led to the greatest thing possible. It led me to understand the power of my own spirit.

I then asked to speak with the higher consciousness of Les to ask questions. Les had mentioned that her left ear was clogged and was becoming an issue. She also had issues with her kidneys.

S: *What is the root cause of the issues with Les's left ear?*

L: We want her to be able to hear our drums, the heartbeat sound that she can hear now because of the clogged ear. We are drumming with her. We will always be guiding her, and we are so grateful to her for sharing our message. We are always there for you, Les, drumming with every heartbeat, with every breath.

S: *Is there anything else you want her to understand about this?*

L: No, we can release the clog now that she understands.

S: *What was the root cause of the issues with her kidneys?*

L: It is from the pain she has taken on that many from that life have taken on; the pain from the Earth, the pain from her people, the repressed anger. It's time for her to let this go. She doesn't need this pain any longer.

S: *Do other people have kidney issues because of the Trail of Tears?*

L: Yes, many and from many other lifetimes of watching the Earth in pain. It's time to let this go. Let go of the pains of the world, let go. This is a new time. A time for healing.

S: Could you heal her kidneys now that she has gotten out this story and she understands that she needs to let this go now?

L: Yes, we are healing her. Her kidneys are already looking better. We are releasing the anger, the fear, the stuck energy, and energetically bringing her body back into a state of harmony.

S: Is there a way to find Aniwaya if I were to look for him?

L: Yes, but understand that Aniwaya's name was changed to Chief Billy Justice by the White Men. The name Justice was actually just a translation from a Cherokee name that meant justice. The White Men called him Billy because of his trip to England where he tried to sign the treaty and so they called him Billy Justice.

S: Is there any other evidence of him anywhere?

L: There were two commissioned paintings of him and his friend Black Fox, but those paintings were done when they were in England and much younger. We will lead you to these pictures.

S: Is there anything else that Aniwaya would like to say?

L: Sometimes the inner journey can be lonely but understand that deep within yourself, within the inner mind, there is more love than you can possibly imagine. So, to those humans on this path, we wish to say that by turning away the ways of the world that you thought you knew, you fall forever into the wellspring of love, which is endless and infinite in its vastness and its expression. But one needs to release the world to fall into it because it is not of this world. This love was used to create this Earth and everything within, but the dynamics and the ways of the world are just the movement and mechanisms of how that love manifests itself. By releasing the world you thought you knew and going inward to the world that is real, you become the embodiment of that love. You become the reflection of that love, and so it's a paradox that you would give up the ways of the world to understand and become the mechanism of the creation of the world.

S: Is there anything humans can do to right the wrongs of history? How can humanity move past all of these wrong doings done to their own people?

L: It's not your place to remove all the negative energy of the world. But what we will say is that for the majority of souls upon the planet, when they leave their physical life, they leave it behind with little left to show for it. They have taken the memories, the experiences back to what you call the in between of lives and it is added to the overall experience of life and creation. Then that soul or that spirit takes the imprint and moves on with it. **However, those that have worked to achieve spiritual mastery and have moved their awareness into their spiritual body and developed it to the point of magnetism do so so that when they leave this Earth, that imprint of that magnetism stays and stays self-aware within itself and has its own consciousness. That is what a human can do, we say, work on yourselves. Achieve peace and harmony as well as spiritual mastery within yourself and your experience will imprint itself into the consciousness of the planet and allow itself to be used as an elevation of consciousness that will be tapped into and carried forth.** This is much like the energetic imprint of Christ, or Buddha, or others who have achieved mastery within their own path and brought a message. Through their internal development they develop their spiritual body such that when they leave the plane of the Earth, their consciousness moves within the framework of that spiritual reality and continues and carries on. While the physical body has left, the spiritual consciousness and reality of what that was, maintains its presence in the consciousness. It has left an indelible imprint which still affects things to this day. And to that extent, that consciousness remains self-aware of itself within its own growth and evolution of the soul. Self-mastery, fully understanding oneself, is not just another experience, but it is an imprint or a pathway, which has been carved into the consciousness and elevates all consciousness afterwards.

S: *So, a soul that chooses self-mastery affects the consciousness of this planet. How does that affect that negative polarity? Is there a battle between the two of these types of imprints, or are they unrelated?*

L: They are diametrically opposed to each other, but also evenly balanced. So where one gains ground, the other comes back into balance. It is a dance that goes back and forth. But within that opposition, you have physical creation, and you have the lessons of experience. You have growth and destruction, death and rebirth, evolution, and change. You have evolutionary opportunities which come to pass in unique ways which may not have existed before on the planet. And so, you have a higher degree of souls which are seeking to incarnate to have the opportunity of that experience and the perils of it in order to either remember or forget. It is the hope of remembering which does not always happen. And sometimes, the trials and tribulations of life take root over the seat of the soul. And that individual may not reach their full potential because they do not remember, they got caught up in the ways of world.

S: *What happens to a soul that comes in, they try to remember, they don't make the shift, they perish? What happens to that soul?*

L: They just carry on. There is nothing that is lost, and much is gained. There may be ramifications and repercussions that they then need to work through or resolve but it just carries on in the greater scheme of things. They move on with their own personal evolution.

S: *How does the story of Aniwaya and the other stories help others to heal?*

L: It has to do with the ability for consciousness to spread. For example, when there is a sick plant, the healthy plants are aware of the sick plant and will release chemicals to enhance its immune system and project healing onto the sick plant. The group elevates that sick plant to help it heal itself and bring it back into balance. And so, it's the same process through the hearing of the recollection of the pain that allows it to be released. It's the same kind of mechanism but applied through consciousness. And as this pain is released from the humans that read this book, this pain is also released from the Earth. This is one of the most divine plans for your books.

S: *Thank you, any final messages?*

L: **We knew there would be destruction and difficulty, but we knew there would be triumph and growth, and we knew that this would be the trail for the human being to take back their freedom once and for all** and live freely again off the Earth, in ALL of her glory. This was always the end goal.

LOOKING FOR ANIWAYA

How do you search for someone who lived over 200 years ago? We weren't sure where to begin; all we had was his Native American name, Aniwaya, and the name the White Men had eventually changed it to, Chief Billy Justice. We knew he walked the Trail of Tears (from where he communicated with us) but we didn't know much else. Suddenly, we had an idea.

Les closed her eyes, and focused on his face, not channeling a memory per se, for it was not an actual memory, but a feeling... Les knew Aniwaya's face when she saw it in the memory of her heart, and, taking a pen to paper and drawing down what she saw, we had our first real clue, his picture.

Using that image, we scoured the internet, looking at photo after photo of Native American warriors, chiefs, family men, providers, hoping we would find a likeness to Les's drawling. Suddenly, we had a match.

An unnamed, decorated, handsome man stood stoically in the photo, the caption beneath it explaining that this man had taken a trip to England with a man named Black Fox. This was incredible information, but nothing could have prepared for what we learned next. As we were searching for records and scouring the internet, Les logged in through ancestry.com and learned that she was blood related to a Chief Billy Justice.

Could this mean that Aniwaya was related to Les? A past life reemerging many, many generations later to tell the stories of the ones before... could it be? I began to wonder, are we just all back again now, carrying countless messages from the past, ready to be heard, ready to be released, so that we can all move into this better future?

Below are some of the drawings that Les drew after her hypnosis sessions and the pictures on the internet that we found using these.

Here is the first picture that Les drew as she focused on Aniwaya's face.

Second picture Les drew of Aniwaya.

Third picture that Les drew that included scenes that she could remember from the past life walking the Trail of Tears.

The picture that Aniwaya said we would find matched up with the face that Les drew.

The two portraits of Cherokee Indians were commissioned by John Hunter and were painted by William Hodges RA in England.

The two Cherokee Indians 375 FIG. I Cherokee Indian (RCS, Hunterian Collection, No 245). Oil on canvas, by William Hodges RA, unsigned. This Indian wears a dark blue blanket with red and yellow braids over a white frilled shirt with a black neckcloth. On his chest is a silver gorget. He has silver wheel earrings, a silver band on his right arm, and a white feather in his hair. Each ear lobe, from which a silver wheel-like ornament hangs, has a hole large enough to pass one or two fingers. It was not unusual for these Indians to pierce their ear lobes with a scalping knife and to stretch the rim of each ear, making the opening larger.

A picture of a man named Black Fox who was traveling with Aniwaya

Information gathered from a number of sources suggests that the two Cherokee Indians whose portraits are above in the Hunterian Collection were the Cherokee chiefs who accompanied W A Bowles to London.

ef William 'Billy' Justice

This is the only picture of a man named Chief Billy Justice that we could find.

Donations to the Cherokee Nation can be sent to
www.cherokeenationfoundation.org

ABOUT THE AUTHOR

Sarah Breskman Cosme is the best-selling author of *A Hypnotist's Journey to Atlantis* and the author of *A Hypnotist's Journey to the Secrets of the Sphinx*. Sarah is a Master Hypnotist, a Level 3 practitioner of Dolores Cannon's QHHT, and a student of Dr. Brian Weiss. With a passion for revealing hidden or undiscovered knowledge vital to the enlightenment of humanity, Sarah continues to speak about her work worldwide.

Sarah earned her bachelor's in Psychology at Northeastern University in Boston MA. After graduation, she worked as a counselor in a halfway house for the mentally ill. "I saw firsthand how the conventional treatment for the mentally ill with medication and talk therapy was not always effective, and I wished that there was something more that I could offer my clients." As a result, Sarah pursued Hypnotherapy, a therapy that uses the subconscious mind to change limiting beliefs and unwanted behavior.

Sarah became a Master Hypnotist in 2009 after which she trained with Dr. Brian Weiss to be a certified Past life Regressionist. Sarah then went on to train with Dolores Cannon's daughter, Julia Cannon, learning her specialized method called Quantum Healing Hypnosis Technique. After many years of dedication and receiving the coveted level 3 practitioner status, Sarah assisted in teaching with Dolores Cannon's daughter Julia all over the world. Sarah has been practicing hypnosis and the "healing arts" for over 12 years.

"I have always been passionate about helping others develop tools that allow them to overcome their difficulties. We are all connected, and by helping one person, we help all people."

For permission, serialization, condensation, adaptions, or other publications, write to the author at https://www.theholistichypnotist.com